Franco Sonzogni

Applying Data Governance practices in the Oil & Gas Upstream

Franco Sonzogni

Applying Data Governance practices in the Oil & Gas Upstream

Towards a strategy that accelerates innovation through efficient data asset management

ScienciaScripts

Imprint
Any brand names and product names mentioned in this book are subject to trademark, brand or patent protection and are trademarks or registered trademarks of their respective holders. The use of brand names, product names, common names, trade names, product descriptions etc. even without a particular marking in this work is in no way to be construed to mean that such names may be regarded as unrestricted in respect of trademark and brand protection legislation and could thus be used by anyone.

Cover image: www.ingimage.com

This book is a translation from the original published under ISBN 978-620-0-42704-5.

Publisher:
Sciencia Scripts
is a trademark of
International Book Market Service Ltd., member of OmniScriptum Publishing Group
17 Meldrum Street, Beau Bassin 71504, Mauritius
Printed at: see last page
ISBN: 978-620-2-75864-2

PROJECT PROFILE

- *Implementation of data governance practices in critical processes of the Santa Cruz de la Southern Oil Company -*

STUDENT

Franco David Sonzogni

CAREER

Specialization in Technology Management

Final work

TUTOR

Gabriel Cuello

YEAR

2013

UNPA

Universidad Nacional de la Patagonia Austral

TABLE OF CONTENTS

INTRODUCTION

By way of introduction, we will mention some of the concepts that are the pillars of the project that we will present below:

1.1 DATA MANAGEMENT AND DATA GOVERNANCE

DATA MANAGEMENT: *Data resource management is the development and implementation of architectures, policies, practices, and procedures that appropriately manage the needs of an enterprise's entire data lifecycle.* [1].

DATA GOVERNANCE: *It is a practice that establishes rules and recommendations to create, process, manipulate and store business data; supported by guidelines in dimensions of: processes, organization/people and IT aspects.* [2].

Data Management and Data Governance offer us the conceptual framework of the new technologies that we want to introduce in the Organisation. In section **[5.3.2.2]** we develop these concepts further.

1.2 PROCESS MANAGEMENT

BUSINESS PROCESS MANAGEMENT (**BPM**) : This is the *name given to the corporate methodology whose objective is to improve the performance (Efficiency and Effectiveness) of the Organisation through the management of business processes, which must be designed, modelled, organised, documented and optimised continuously. The Process Management Model refers to the operational change of the company by migrating from a functional operation to a process management operation.* [3].

BUSINESS PROCESS MODEL AND NOTATION (**BPMN**): *This is the name given to the standardised graphic notation that allows the modelling of business processes, in a workflow format (workflows). The main objective of BPMN is to provide a standard notation that is easily readable and understandable by all those involved and interested in the business (internal and external customers).* [4].

BPM and BPMN offer us a set of techniques and tools that facilitate the classification, characterisation and measurement of the business processes that we will achieve with this project. These are present in the culture of the organisation and are applied naturally in the management of its processes [5]. The definition of critical processes of the Asset is given by the impact that these can generate on the business strategy and the results. In this case the focus will be on data management activities, information generation and decision making.

Through BPM techniques and methodologies, the analysis of the activities involved in the processes will be deepened in order to obtain and formalize the following elements of analysis [6]:

- ✓ **Input and output elements associated with the activities with the identification of suppliers and customers respectively.**
- ✓ **Map of the processes, schematised by means of BPMN.**
- ✓ **Matrix showing the degree of responsibility of the actors involved.**
- ✓ **Objective and scope of the processes.**
- ✓ **Metrics that facilitate the measurement of the degree of efficiency with which they are executed.**

All these elements will be input for the analysis that will allow us to define the data governance programme and its elements (See details in section [**5.2.2.1**])

1.3 OTHER CONSIDERATIONS

For the elaboration of this work we not only based on the material seen in the specialization career; we also studied and analyzed theoretical aspects from different and diverse sources associated to the problem that it addresses (included in bibliography). In the region and in our country, the topic is not as mature as it was observed in more developed regions (USA, Canada, UK).

It is also observed that the accelerated evolution of information technologies, the complexity of the context in which businesses are developed and the exponential growth of the volume of information available, will force companies and even the state to have a data strategy that allows them to administer and manage it as a resource. Decisions must be taken more and more quickly and the only way to reduce the uncertainty and risk that this implies is to ensure the availability of data and necessary information, at the right time and in the right form. This undoubtedly raises the need to have a strategy that favours the alignment of the elements involved.

It was considered to give the project the character of a pilot, given that in this format we ensure that it has a good chance of being approved by the committee that will evaluate it. Furthermore, given the characteristics and impact that this type of change generates, we think it is important to acquire, through the execution of the pilot, the necessary experience that will allow us to plan a project of greater scope with greater precision. This will be presented as a "Project Profile". [7]

2 EXECUTIVE SUMMARY

2.1 NAME

The project has been named "***Application of data governance practices in critical production processes for the Santa Cruz Asset of the Petrolera del Sur company***".

2.2 LOCATION & DURATION

This project will be executed in the Santa Cruz Asset, located in the province of Santa Cruz, which is part of the businesses developed by Petrolera del Sur through its business area "Oil or Gas Exploration and Production (E&P)". It will have a total duration of four years.

2.3 OBJECTIVES AND GOALS OF THE PROJECT

2.3.1 OVERALL OBJECTIVES

The general objectives of the project are:

I. Acquire and certify knowledge associated with data management practices and methodologies.
II. With the support of external consultancy; design a data governance programme for the business processes considered critical and plan its deployment
III. Deploy the data governance programme for the processes achieved by the project.
IV. Measure the benefits of the project.
V. Evaluate, document and disseminate the results obtained.

2.3.2 SPECIFIC OBJECTIVES / GOALS

We will now group together the specific objectives and targets associated with each of the general objectives:

I. Acquire and certify knowledge associated with data management practices and methodologies:

- ✓ **Acquire the appropriate training material for certification.**
- ✓ **Provide the necessary resources to enable the designated staff to implement the training activities.**
- ✓ **To certify the knowledge acquired by the staff through the verification of the Institute for the Certification of Computing Professionals (ICCP[1])**

II. With the support of external consultancy; design a data governance system for the business processes considered critical and plan its deployment

- ✓ **Hire the service of external consultancy. Include clear specifications for contracting. Ensure the consultant's experience in data governance system design and implementation processes.**
- ✓ **Document and formalize the survey of the processes achieved.**
- ✓ **Design Data Strategy, include all components defined by the model applied and consider the initial assessment (Gaps) of the situation of the Assets in terms of Data Governance. *See detailed project profile for more details.***
- ✓ **Review and approve the deployment schedule for the data governance system.**

III. Deploy the data governance system for the processes defined in the project scope.

- ✓ **Adequate critical contracts reached by the data governance programme (DGP).**

[1] The mission of the ICCP is promoting the continuous improvement of the Information and Systems professions and professionals through certification, enforcement of a professional code of ethics, standards of conduct, and continuing education.

- ✓ **Adequate roles and functions reached by the PGD.**
- ✓ **Application of PGD in "Process of determining and monitoring the causes of production losses" and reduce the impact of gas production losses on potential production of the same product to 7%. Reduce the impact of oil and gasoline losses on potential production of the same product to 9%. At the end of the project, increase gas sales by 2% and oil and gasoline sales by 24%.**
- ✓ **Application of PGD in "Production monitoring and control process".**
- ✓ **Application of PGD in "Process of diffusion and dissemination of production". At the end of the project it must be possible to calculate zero risk in terms of the possibility of non-compliance with internal and external regulations to the Asset regarding the notification and dissemination of the production.**
- ✓ **Application of PGD in "Process of monitoring and control of costs associated with production".**

IV. Measure the benefits of the project.

- ✓ **Design and implement a control panel to monitor the variables associated with the project benefits. Both the quantitative and qualitative ones.**
- ✓ **Define a strategy for communicating the results.**

V. Evaluate, document and disseminate the results obtained.

- ✓ **Make a critical analysis of the project's implementation and results.**
- ✓ **Assess the feasibility of implementing new projects associated with data management.**
- ✓ **Document and formalize the results.**
- ✓ **Disseminate results at the company level.**

2.4 PROJECT BENEFICIARIES

We will classify the beneficiaries of the project into internal and external, as well as direct and indirect. The criterion of internal and external is with respect to the area in which one acts with respect to the organization of the Asset. As regards the criteria of direct and indirect beneficiaries, the fundamentals are as follows

- ➢ **Direct beneficiaries**: Within this group of beneficiaries we will find all the clients of the project, either internal or external to the Asset, who will perceive during and after the execution of the project, qualitative or quantitative benefits that will have a direct influence on the results of the activity they develop.
- ➢ **Indirect beneficiaries**: This group includes all the project's customers who will perceive improvements in the data and information consumption processes without these necessarily impacting on their activities.

In Table 1 we can see the beneficiaries identified and classified with the above-mentioned criteria:

Table 1: Beneficiaries identified for the project

Internos al Activo		Externos al Activo	
Directos	Indirectos	Directos	Indirectos
Gerencia de Activo Gerencia de Operaciones Contratistas		Gerencia de producción de Petrolera del Sur Gestores de datos Petrolera del Sur Organismos públicos de control y fiscalización	
Proveedores	Administradores y fiscales de contratos MACS - Medio Ambiente, Calidad y Seguridad Socios	Auditorias y Control de Petrolera del Sur	Gerencia de servicios TICs Petrolera del Sur Gerencia de finanzas Petrolera del Sur Gerencia de contratos y abastecimientos Petrolera del Sur Gestores de proyectos de Petrolera del Sur

Note: Source: The data displayed in the table are produced by the company.

2.5 PROJECT COSTS

2.5.1 FIXED INVESTMENT

Table 2 details the amounts of fixed investment. These are classified according to the concept of the investment.

Table 2: Details of fixed investment required to implement the project

Concepto de Inversión fija / Detalles	Monto U$S (Dólares)
Formación (1)	
Gestor de datos - Activo Santa Cruz	4,000
Gestor de datos - Gerencia de producción Compania	4,000
Gestor de datos - Otro Activo	4,000
Analista funcional TI	4,000
Sub total Formación	**16,000**
Consultoría Externa (2)	
Consultoría etapa 1	66,900
Consultoría etapa 2	66,900
Sub total Consultoría Externa	**133,800**
Servicios TI (3)	
Analista consultor de procesos	4,700
Analista consultor especialista	10,000
Analista funcional	36,000
Sub total Servicios TI	**50,700**
Logística (4)	
Viajes	20,800
Estadía	46,800
Capacitación	1,500
Sub total Logística	**69,100**
Total inversión fija	**269,600**

Note: Source: The data displayed in the table are produced by the company.

The project's income was quantified according to the increase in product sales resulting from the reduction in production losses.

2.5.2 CASH FLOW

In Table 3 and based on all the data presented above, the cash flow of the project is presented.

Table 3: Project cash flow. Expressed in dollars [U$S] for periods of one year

Concepto / Detalle	Año 1	Año 2	Año 3	Año 4
Ingresos				
Capital inicial invertido	269,600	0	0	0
Saldo año anterior	0	137,467	102,933	400,960
Ventas de Gas	0	0	793,354	574,928
Ventas de petróleo y gasolina	0	0	2,266,082	1,300,652
Total de Ingresos	269,600	137,467	3,162,370	2,276,539
Gastos				
Inversión	132,133	34,533	102,933	0
Gastos de producción	0	0	2,025,265	1,378,345
Total gastos	132,133	34,533	2,128,199	1,378,345
Impuestos				
Regalias [12%]	0	0	367,132	225,069
Ingresos Brutos [1%]	0	0	30,594	18,756
Ganancias [37%]	0	0	235,484	93,761
Total Impuestos	0	0	633,211	337,587
Saldo a ser transferido	**137,467**	**102,933**	**400,960**	**560,607**

Note: Source: The data displayed in the table are produced by the company.

As can be seen from the table above, the **benefits of the project at the end of the project will be a cash balance of US$560,607 or its equivalent in national currency**.

2.6 FINANCIAL EVALUATION INDICES

2.6.1 NET PRESENT VALUE

Applying a discount rate of **15.3%,** the Net Present Value of the project's net benefits amounts to USD **142,065**. The Benefit-Cost ratio gives a coefficient of **1.05**. Table 4 provides details of the values underlying the above values.

Table 4: Financial Evaluation [US$ amounts] - Net Present Value. Discount rate 15.3%.

Año	Valores sin descontar			Valores descontados		
	Costos	Beneficios	Beneficios Netos	Costos	Beneficios	Beneficios Netos
0	16,000	0	-16,000	16,000	0	-16,000
1	116,133	0	-116,133	100,723	0	-100,723
2	34,533	0	-34,533	25,976	0	-25,976
3	2,761,410	3,059,436	298,027	1,801,536	1,995,968	194,432
4	1,715,932	1,875,579	159,648	970,918	1,061,251	90,333
Total	4,644,008	4,935,015	291,007	2,915,153	3,057,219	142,065
	Relación Beneficio/Costo	1.05	VAN	142,065	TIR	56.5%

Note: Source: The data displayed in the table are produced by the company.

2.6.2 TIR - INTERNAL RATE OF RETURN

The project's internal rate of return is **56.5%**. Table 4 shows the values considered in the calculation.

2.7 CONCLUSIONS AND RECOMMENDATIONS

The proposed project incorporates, formalizes and promotes data management practices that will allow Activo Santa Cruz and the Southern Oil Company to obtain improvements in management and results.

The profit trigger is based on the reduction of production losses and their consequent impact on production increases. It also represents the point of greatest sensitivity of the project. We recommend carrying out a sensitivity analysis if you decide to implement it.

This project will lay the foundation for the development of data management as a necessary and fundamental discipline for achieving business objectives at all levels of the organization.

The scenario described represents a favourable environment; the Asset and the Company have the necessary strengths to exploit all the opportunities that were dimensioned in this project. The weaknesses and threats were considered in the design of this project and do not represent risks that prevent its execution.

It seems that we recommend to execute the project in Activo Santa Cruz, we consider that there is a suitable environment for its execution. It is also profitable because it has a **NPV (Net Present Value) of US$ 142,065,** a benefit-cost ratio of US$ **1.05 and** an **IRR of 56.5%**.

3 PROJECT PROFILE

3.1 NAME AND BACKGROUND OF THE PROJECT

3.1.1 NAME OF THE PROJECT

The project has been named "***Application of data governance practices in critical production processes for the Santa Cruz Asset of the Petrolera del Sur company***".

3.1.2 NEED OR NEEDS TO BE SOLVED

Over the last three years, the Petrolera del Sur company has been addressing the issue of data management as an aspect that requires special attention within the work processes. Decisions have been made in this area that have allowed for the improvement of different problems associated with the subject. Specific initiatives have been carried out within the organisation of Activo Santa Cruz, the most important of which were

- **Creation and incorporation of the role of "Data Manager" within the organizational structure** [8].
- **Review and adaptation of critical work processes focusing on the optimization of data flows.** [8].
- **Extension of the functional scope of the technological tools involved in information management.** [9].
- **Integration of data between different areas and disciplines**

The development of all these initiatives, the desire for continuous improvement and the evolution achieved by the changes made generated new needs that we intend to address with this project. These are:

- **Continue to innovate by acquiring and applying new knowledge in data management.**
- **A framework needs to be formalised to facilitate the establishment of data policies strategically aligned with the company's goals.**
- **We consider, based on our experience and case studies, the need to establish formal data governance practices in critical Asset processes.** [8], [2] y [10].
- **Formal measurement criteria need to be established in the application and evolution of the data practices and policies implemented.** [11] y [12].

3.1.2.1 ABOUT NEW KNOWLEDGE

It is known that the introduction of new management methodologies are also alternatives that promote and facilitate innovation within organizations[2][13]. Petrolera del Sur is aware of the progress made in data management. In this instance, with some evidence that supports the benefit that can be generated by the formal treatment of these issues in the areas of management and business strategy, it is intended to deepen and extend the scope of the application of techniques and practices associated with data management. Currently, the Company as a whole recognises the need to have a framework that is based on a body of recognised, proven and applicable knowledge to the organisational culture. Considering Activo Santa Cruz as a pioneer in these issues, it is proposed to implement a pilot project in the same.
Three alternatives were considered viable to meet the need:

1) **Hire specific consulting services that transmit experience and knowledge within the organization.**
2) **Train and certify our own staff.**
3) **A combination of alternatives one and two.**

---

[2] FERNANDEZ CIRELLI, A. (1996). *The Technological Entrepreneur*. Chapter 1, Page 22: "There is a wide range of technological possibilities associated with management methods, commercialisation, distribution, etc. These are also transformation technologies, although in this case it is not so simple to measure the impact of the applied knowledge". EUDEBA.

The project considers alternative 3.

3.1.2.2 ABOUT THE DATA MANAGEMENT FRAMEWORK

There is a framework in place that promotes practices and processes aimed at treating data as an important element. However, there are still many aspects to be improved, in some cases the informality of existing means is an obstacle to achieving greater awareness and strengthening of the elements involved. When analyzing the context of this problem at a global level, we found experiences and research that resulted in the generation of knowledge associated with this problem, we discovered that these same concerns and needs were raised by different organizations, this is not a new issue. Thus, there is currently what is called a body of formal knowledge that seeks to maintain and generate a set of concepts and theoretical elements that put and value data management as a discipline. We refer specifically to: "*The DAMA Guide to The Data Management Body of Knowledge - DAMA-DMBOK Guide*" elaborated and maintained by DAMA[3]. This material is the conceptual basis for defining a framework to suit Petrolera del Sur and Activo Santa Cruz.

3.1.2.3 ABOUT DATA GOVERNANCE

Within the framework that we intend to design and apply to data management, the element or function called "*Data Governance*" is the heart of it. This will specify the policies and principles that will be applied in the strategy defined by this project. Previous internal work and experiences will be considered. Especially the so-called "METHODOLOGY FOR CONTINUOUS IMPROVEMENT OF INFORMATION PROCESSES" of [14].

3.1.2.4 ABOUT THE EVALUATION OF THE APPLIED METHODOLOGIES

In this section we quote again from the book "*The technological entrepreneur*", Chapter 1: "However, *beyond the process or the product itself, there is a wide range of technological possibilities associated with management methods, commercialisation, distribution, etc. These are also transformation technologies, although in this case it is not so simple to measure the impact of the applied knowledge*[4]. " [13]. The author already warns us about the difficulty of evaluating the impact/benefit for this type of initiative, in which innovation is driven by the application of new management methodologies. Nevertheless, we understand that the approach proposed by this project will allow us to evaluate the scenario that represents the starting point (The "How It Is"), taking the dimensions and metrics, which, as it evolves, due to the project's action plan, will allow us to demonstrate the effects of the change generated (The "How It Is"), which will be based on the application of a model known and tested in other organisations. The gap between the two scenarios is to be resolved.

3.1.3 PROJECT BENEFICIARIES

We will classify the beneficiaries of the project into internal and external, as well as direct and indirect. The criterion of internal and external is with respect to the area in which one acts with respect to the organization of the Asset. As regards the criteria of direct and indirect beneficiaries, the fundamentals are as follows

- **Direct beneficiaries**: Within this group of beneficiaries we will find all the clients of the project, either internal or external to the Asset, who will perceive during and after the execution of the project, qualitative or quantitative benefits that will have a direct influence on the results of the activity they develop.

[3] DAMA International is a non-profit, vendor-independent, global association of technical and business professionals dedicated to advancing the concepts and practices of information and data management.

[4] FERNANDEZ CIRELLI, A. (1996). The Technological Entrepreneur. EUDEBA.

- **Indirect beneficiaries**: This group includes all the project's customers who will perceive improvements in the data and information consumption processes without these necessarily impacting on their activities.

In Table 5 we can see the beneficiaries identified and classified with the above-mentioned criteria:

Table 5: Beneficiaries identified for the project, by location with respect to the Asset and by the form of benefit they will experience with the project

Internos al Activo		Externos al Activo	
Directos	Indirectos	Directos	Indirectos
Gerencia de Activo Gerencia de Operaciones Contratistas		Gerencia de producción de Petrolera del Sur Gestores de datos Petrolera del Sur Organismos públicos de control y fiscalización	
Proveedores	Administradores y fiscales de contratos MACS - Medio Ambiente, Calidad y Seguridad Socios	Auditorias y Control de Petrolera del Sur	Gerencia de servicios TICs Petrolera del Sur Gerencia de finanzas Petrolera del Sur Gerencia de contratos y abastecimientos Petrolera del Sur Gestores de proyectos de Petrolera del Sur

Note: Source: The data displayed in the table are produced by the company.

3.1.4 BENEFICIARIES' OPINION OF THE PROJECT

The management style with which the Asset executes its business strategy is widely favourable to the application of new work methodologies that tend to improve performance indicators. As for the subject that summons us, we have already mentioned some initiatives that have been carried out and which amply demonstrate the interest in maintaining an innovative conduct in this respect.
Of the initiatives implemented, all impacted on the improvement of workflows in which critical Asset data is manipulated. This contributed to awaken the interest of the different actors involved in the processes, in great measure because they were the first to notice the benefits, in general this allowed them to better develop their tasks. These benefits are associated with:

- Considerable reduction of the time they use to process, classify and obtain the data necessary for decision making.
- Reduction of re-work due to redundant data maintenance
- Greater use of the information technologies involved in the work processes.
- A greater integration of the data managed by the different disciplines was achieved, which favoured the creation of collaborative work environments and the critical analysis inherent in business management.
- It promoted the alignment of the Asset strategy with people's individual objectives.
- The risk of problems associated with data quality was reduced.

Another aspect that indicates the favourable opinion of the beneficiaries of the project; is given by the fact that in the different audits associated with critical aspects of the management, the results obtained in the final reports, have positively weighted the importance that the Asset gives to the efficient management of the information.
Within the management style mentioned above, one aspect to highlight is the generation of different formal and collaborative (Multidisciplinary) spaces for discussion and critical analysis of the results. These spaces

favour the execution of activities related to the integration of the data, while generating consensus as to the characteristics and ways in which the information should be presented and followed up. The impact and importance of planning and managing the use of the information began to be perceived and recognized. Figure 1 shows the management model, as seen from its analysis spaces.

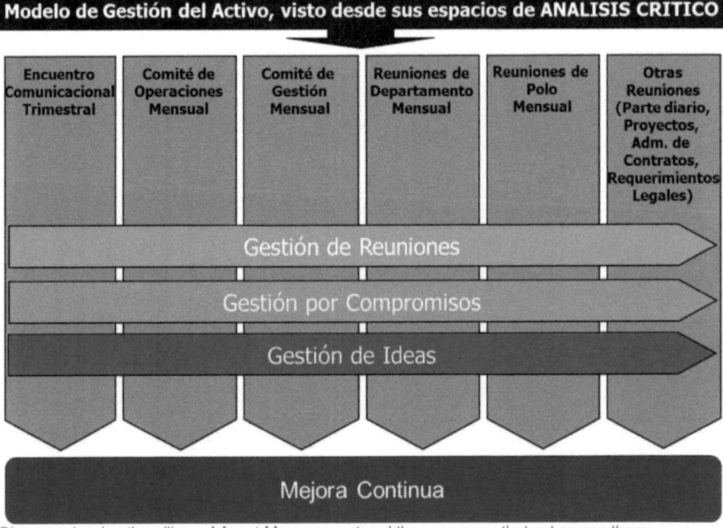

Figure 1: Diagram showing the pillars of Asset Management and the processes that cut across them.
Source: Obtained from the analyses carried out. Own elaboration.

The benefits identified largely relate to the alignment of data handling with this mode of management. In this sense, a lot of work was done on the data consumption processes and on the modelling by means of IT tools of[5] solutions that favour the availability of information in time and form for each of the analysis spaces indicated in the figure.

Another aspect to highlight is the greater integration between the business areas and the information technology area. By creating the role of data manager on the business side, new communication channels were created that favour the alignment of the strategies of each of these areas. This is perceived and has generated new areas of communication, in which this problem is recognised as being of growing importance and it is understood that it must be tackled as a whole.

In short, all the aspects and evidence mentioned above give us enough elements to consider promoting this project. We consider that the execution of this project is the natural step that the organization should take to continue materializing a path of continuous improvement in terms of data management.

3.1.5 ENTITY RESPONSIBLE FOR THE PROJECT

The responsibility for the project will lie with the Asset Management, specifically with the Asset Manager. Although it is a project that, depending on the success of its results, can be extended to the rest of the company, in this instance we consider it important to leave its management in the hands of the Asset. The importance lies in taking advantage of the accumulated experience.

[5] IT: Information Technology. It involves computer technology as a whole.

Similarly, it is considered a success factor to include in the work team people who represent other areas of the company that interact with Asset management. It is fundamental to consider aspects that give the final product a global vision that facilitates its replication in the future. In the section on Technical aspects of the project we will give more details.

3.1.6 PREVIOUS OR ONGOING STUDIES

Within the activities of the Asset and the company, studies, evaluations and even publications have been carried out that have been awarded prizes, in terms of data management. The main ones are mentioned below. In the first instance, we will list the studies carried out in a scope that goes beyond the Asset. These are:

- In 2008 Petrolera del Sur is formally recognized for its work and experience in data quality assessment and management. This work was published in written media that value the methodological contribution to address these issues in the oil industry. [9].

- In 2009, Petrolera de Sur, through interdisciplinary work and led by the applied technology area, generated a document called *"METHODOLOGY FOR CONTINUOUS IMPROVEMENT OF INFORMATION PROCESSES",* [14]. This document specifies the processes required for the implementation of Data Governance in the company's Exploration and Production area. This methodology was not applied.

We will now mention the main studies carried out at the Asset level:

- Between 2007 and 2008 a multidisciplinary team, supported by external consultants, carried out a comprehensive evaluation of the assets. The result of this evaluation leads to the presentation of a business case that aims to execute the improvement opportunities identified. What is remarkable about this work is that the evaluation mentions the application of a data management system as one of the elements of solution to the identified shortcomings. [8].

- In 2008, the incorporation of the role of data manager in the Active allowed the execution of a series of analyses focused on data management; this resulted in the development of a set of improvements aimed at optimizing critical data processes, especially in the areas of production and associated with issues of quality, integration, interfaces and reporting of data and information.

- In 2011 a team of professionals and technicians from the Asset under the guidance of a specialist consultant; applies and certifies ISO 9000 quality methodologies for the Asset's laboratory activities. This project showed excellent results in the short term. Data management in each of the laboratory processes was considered with special attention. The quality principles of the ISO 9000 standards and the data management principles to be applied in this project have many points in common.

- Between 2010 and 2011, a multidisciplinary team from the Assets and IT areas will execute a pilot project to apply the process management methodology in one of the production poles. This experience included the application of new technology. During the project there was a strong focus on the efficient management of data and information. Driven by the good results obtained, the intention is to extend the scope of the pilot project to all of the Assets during the 2012 and 2013 periods. [5].

- In 2011 different evaluation models are being analysed to establish the present of the Asset as far as Data Governance is concerned. A model was selected and applied, its result is part of the foundation of this project. The following sections will address this issue in more detail. [15].

3.2 PROJECT CONTEXT

3.2.1 SCOPE - SCOPE OF THE PROJECT

Petrolera del Sur is an energy company that operates in Argentina, carrying out oil and gas exploration and production tasks. The company operates under a concession regime by the provinces or the country over different hydrocarbon producing regions. For this purpose, it has a business area called "Exploration and Production (E&P)", within which it gathers and manages different production units which it calls Assets. The project in question is directed to this area and specifically to the Santa Cruz Asset, which is located within the limits of the province of Santa Cruz. The Asset is made up of companies that share the financial resources needed to develop the activities and also the profits, the companies that make up the Asset are

- HOLY CROSS LOT I
- SANTA CRUZ LOT II
- SANTA CRUZ LOT III

These companies are made up of different concession areas. Although the operations involved in these companies are all assumed by Petrolera del Sur, all the management is adequate to the corporate participation, this is a factor that somehow makes it complex.

The scope of this project is established in the critical production processes of these companies.
The processes considered critical are the following:

- Process of determining and monitoring the causes of production losses.
- Production monitoring and control process.
- Process of diffusion and dissemination of the production.
- Process of monitoring and controlling the costs associated with production.

For all these processes, the following topics will be considered:

- Means of data acquisition and manipulation.
- Roles and functions associated with responsibility for data.
- Formal documentation associated with the impacted processes, focusing on the data elements manipulated.
- Information technology applications involved.
- History of data problems.
- Contracts for products or services associated with the processes.

3.2.1.1 OBJECTIVE - PRODUCTS OR SERVICES OF THE PROJECT

According to the scope and objectives set, the final product of this project will be made up of the following elements:

I. Human Capital

    - Certified data professionals to take responsibility for executing the data governance practice implementation plan.

II. Set of deliverables associated with a data governance system adapted to the work culture of Petrolera del Sur in the Santa Cruz Asset:

    - **Data strategy**: Data management work programme with focus on data governance. It includes a plan to maintain and improve the quality, integrity, security and access to information and data. It should consider the needs inherent in the business strategy of the

Asset and the Company. Responsibility for the programme should be clearly specified. The strategy should contain the following three elements:

A. Document with data governance programme: Includes vision, business case, objectives, metrics, critical success factors, risk identification, etc.
B. Programme Scope Agreement: Goals and objectives defined for the time horizon defined in the programme, roles and organisation required to meet them.
C. Implementation plan: Detailed schedule of activities to be developed, milestones and deadlines for deliverables.

- **Data policies**: A set of declarations and commitments at the organizational level regarding data. It includes the foundations and general rules for the creation, acquisition, integration, security, quality and use of data and information. These must be effectively communicated, monitored, leveraged and frequently reviewed.
- **Data architecture**: Document with a general description of all the elements involved in the data infrastructure of the Asset.
- **Data standard and procedures**: Defines nomenclature standards, data modeling standards, database design, procedures for each data management function. Formalization of documents with methods and techniques followed for specific data management tasks. These must be effectively communicated, monitored, leveraged and reviewed.
- **Strategy for compliance with current regulations**: The data governance methodology to be implemented must contemplate effective compliance with all the regulations in force. A control plan must be specified to facilitate, ensure, document and monitor compliance with all data and information regulations.
- **Management of data subjects**: The way in which all subjects related to data and information management are managed must be specified. Including aspects of:

    - Data quality.
    - Conflicts of nomenclature.
    - Conflicts between business rules. Clarification of doubts.
    - Security, confidentiality and data privacy.
    - Non-compliance with regulations.
    - Non-conformities in relation to policies, standards, architecture and procedures
    - Conflict of interest between data clients.
    - New data requirements.
    - Data migrations.
    - Negotiation and review of data sharing agreements,
    - Etc.

  The control mechanism for the management and monitoring of all data subjects should be included in this deliverable. Consider monitoring using metrics that indicate efficiency.
- **Identification of future projects**: Document with a list of initiatives to improve data and information management. Consider especially aspects of: Data Architecture, Data Warehouse and Business Intelligence, Master Data Management, Meta Data Management and Data Quality.
- **Data valuation strategy**: A document with guidelines and criteria that allow the Asset data to be given a value.
- **Communication strategy**: Document with a proposal of formal and informal means to be used for the communication of issues concerning data management. This strategy must favour efficient communication, both to data and information producers and to consumers, ensuring that everyone understands and is aware of the importance of complying with the data policies defined by the company.
- **Change management strategy**: The project involves reviewing roles and functions, proposing all appropriate changes to the data governance methodology to be implemented.

It is required to provide a plan of activities to be developed throughout the implementation, aimed at mitigating the impact of change.

III. Data governance methodology implemented on the defined processes. Evidence of their application, maintenance, control and measurement of evolution.

3.2.1.2 AREA OF INFLUENCE

The area of greatest impact of the project is undoubtedly the Santa Cruz Asset. To a lesser extent it is also the objective of this project to influence the E&P area of the entire company.
The final product of the project will be deployed on the Asset Management methodology. In Figure 2 we can see a diagram representing the organisational structure of the Asset.

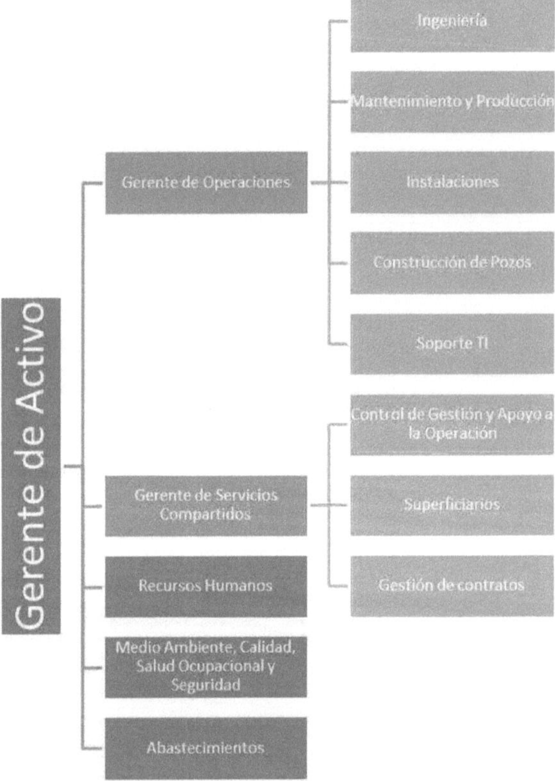

Figure 2: Organizational diagram of the Asset.
Source: Information provided by the human resources area of the company.

The area of the organisation in which this project will have the greatest degree of influence (HIGH) is "*Operations Management*". Most of the data handling activities associated with the processes achieved are

carried out in this area. Other clients of the project in which it is expected to have a significant influence are those who consume data and information originating from these processes. On the rest of the clients, the project will have less influence (MEDIA).
In Table 6 we show a scheme that represents the different levels of influence of the project (*High and Medium*) considering the classification of project beneficiaries we made in due course and also the considerations mentioned above.

Table 6: Beneficiaries identified for the project classified by level of influence

	Internos al Activo		Externos al Activo	
Nivel de Influencia	Directos	Indirectos	Directos	Indirectos
Alta	Gerencia de Activo Gerencia de Operaciones Contratistas		Gerencia de producción de Petrolera del Sur Gestores de datos Petrolera del Sur Organismos públicos de control y fiscalización	
Media	Proveedores	Administradores y fiscales de contratos MACS - Medio Ambiente, Calidad y Seguridad Socios	Auditorias y Control de Petrolera del Sur	Gerencia de servicios TICs Petrolera del Sur Gerencia de finanzas Petrolera del Sur Gerencia de contratos y abastecimientos Petrolera del Sur Gestores de proyectos de Petrolera del Sur

Note: Source: Obtained from the analysis carried out. The data shown in the table are produced by the company.

3.2.1.3 PROJECT LIFETIME

The duration of this project is set at four years. While theory and good practice recommend a life span of no less than five years for this type of initiative, we believe that there is a time gain in terms of Petrolera del Sur's and Activo Santa Cruz's track record. We consider the road travelled as time gained.
The life of the project will be divided into different phases, which will be ordered by a schedule of activities that considers all the aspects associated with the project. In the following sections we will expand on this.

3.2.2 STUDY OF THE CURRENT SITUATION

In this section we will concentrate the analysis on the current situation (The "How it is"), focusing on the internal organisation of the Asset and on the issues concerning data governance. We will take as a starting point for this analysis the definition of the concept / function "Data Governance"; we will cite the most widespread and influential ones at present, these are

> *"An official orchestration / alignment of people, processes and*
> *The technology to enable an organisation to manage its data as a business asset".*
>
> **- The MDM Institute -** [16]

"Data governance is defined as the processes, policies, standards, organisation and technologies required to manage and ensure the availability, accessibility, quality, consistency, auditability and security of an enterprise or institution's data".

- Information Technology - [16]

"Data governance encompasses the people, processes and technology needed to create a consistent business view, managing data for the purpose of

Increase consistency and confidence in decision making
Reduce the risk of regulatory fines
Improve data security.
Achieving information quality throughout the organization.
Maximize income.
Designate responsibility for information management".

- Wikipedia - [16]

"Data governance is a quality control discipline, which aims to add new rigour and discipline to the process of managing, using, improving and protecting organisational information. Effective data management can improve the quality, availability and integrity of an organisation's data by fostering collaboration between all levels of the organisation and a supportive policy structure.

- IBM - [16]

"Data governance is a system of decision making and accountability for information and related processes, executed according to models that describe what actions to take, with what information and when, in what circumstances and by what methods.

- The Data Governance Institute - [16]

Considering each of the definitions and according to the background we cited in the previous sections, we can infer that in the company and in the Assets, there are already many of the elements mentioned in the different definitions cited. Perhaps the biggest shortcoming is found in the informality and lack of a comprehensive view of the problem. When we mention informality as one of the interfering aspects, we mean the following:

- Formally, there is no integrated data strategy containing a work plan that favours an adequate alignment of processes, people and technology. Although there is an IT - E&P Committee within the company, and in some way this would have responsibility for designing and executing these types of activities, experience indicates that it has not been able to do so. The committee lacks the institutional recognition it deserves and does not yet have the power to influence strategic decision making.
- For many of the critical data handling processes, there are no processes that indicate minimum criteria of quality, responsibility and control. Informally, procedures and instructions generated by specific areas of the organisation are disseminated without following any specific criteria.
- For many of the critical Asset processes, there are not yet formal plans to indicate what steps to take when data problems arise. Those that do exist aim to comply with current legal regulations and others to address the company's own needs.
- Informally, there are data integration rules between different disciplines or areas of the organization. Formally, documentation is only generated at the level of requirements of the IT areas and for specific projects in which technological solutions that integrate data are generated.

The comprehensive view in terms of data has evolved considerably in recent years. Progress in this area has been uneven, with some areas of the company more aware than others.
As mentioned in previous sections, initiatives have been developed in the field of Assets that have significantly favoured the promotion of projects of this type.
The experience of leading organisations in formally applying data management methodologies suggests starting small, with limited-scope pilot projects that facilitate early wins and promote continuity of larger projects. It is also essential to continue to implement a strategy associated with the topic (while recognizing that it can change), beyond administrative and organizational[6] changes.
Within the analysis and study activities preliminary to the project, different evaluation models were considered that would allow us to determine the current situation of the Asset in aspects of data governance. Of the different alternatives considered, the one developed by the company KALIDO[7] was selected, which is called the "*Kalido Data Governance Maturity Model*".
The application of this model allows us to have a starting point that facilitates the interpretation of the current scenario. We will now present the results.

3.2.2.1 MATURITY IN GOVERNANCE OF ASSET DATA SANTA CRUZ[8]

3.2.2.1.1 INTRODUCTION

Like any major business capability, data governance requires the right organisation, processes and technology to be successful. Adopting the right methodology does not happen overnight [17], [18], [19], [20], [21], [22], [23], [24], [25] y [26]. Kalido's data governance maturity model is based on market research within more than forty companies at different stages of maturity. In this model we have the following stages of maturity (Stages):

1. **Focused on IT applications,**
2. **Focused on the Company's data repositories,**
3. **Policy focus**
4. **Widely regulated.**

These statuses are assigned according to the evolution shown by the organizations in terms of how their data is treated. At the same time, the "*Kalido Data Governance Maturity Model*" is prescriptive, as it provides organizational, process and technology aspects that must be aligned to move to a higher level of maturity (Next Step). Table 7 shows the classification and characterisation of the four stages of the Kalido model according to the three data governance elements to be considered in the analysis (Organisation, Processes and Technology).

Table 7: Classification and characterisation of each of the elements of analysis achieved by the stages proposed by the Kalido model

	Etapa 1	**Etapa 2**	**Etapa 3**	**Etapa 4**
Organización	*Nada*	*Localizado*	*En Formación*	*Permanente*
Procesos	*Nada*	*Informal*	*Definidos*	*Optimizados*
Tecnología	*Transacción*	*Dato*	*Política de Datos*	*Impulsada por Políticas.*
	Centrado en las aplicaciones TI	**Centrado en los repositorios de datos de la Empresa**	**Centrado en las Políticas**	**Ampliamente regulados**

[6] Translated from: DGI. (08 of 11 of 2014). *The Data Governance Institute (DGI).* Retrieved 05 of 05 of 2013, from The Data Governance Institute (DGI): http://www.datagovernance.com/

[7] Kalido is one of the leading providers of information management software. Kalido enables companies to manage data as an asset by supporting data management business processes. Unlike traditional approaches that treat the symptoms of bad information, Kalido addresses the cause, keeping bad data out of the business environment. The result is better data to improve business performance.

[8] Copyright © 2010 Kalido

Note: Source: Translated from WINSTON, CHEN. (2010). *Kalido Data Governance Maturity Model.* Information received by email

Next we will characterize each of the stages.

3.2.2.1.2 STEP 1 - FOCUS ON IT APPLICATIONS

In stage one of the maturity model presented here, we refer to a scenario in which the organisation has widely adopted technology for data processing. The information systems were designed to support the business transactions. The data is seen as a sub-product of the business operation and is not given a value that is beyond the transaction and the application that processed it. Data is not treated as a valuable, shared asset. The need to govern data is not yet recognised. At this stage success in efficiently managing data is limited, mainly for two reasons:

1. *Improvement efforts are driven by the IT area and without adequate business support.*
2. *The limited flexibility offered by packaged applications.*

The data governance elements at this stage have the following characteristic:

Organization: The authority and responsibility for the data does not exist. There is a clear separation between IT and business and little collaboration between the two. The business assumes that the responsibility for the data is IT's.

Processes: There are no processes for data governance.

Technology: The data models and the business processes with their rules are embedded in the IT applications. There are no tools to model, manage and assure the quality of the data. There is little data integration between different sectors of the organisation.

3.2.2.1.3 STEP 2 - FOCUS ON ENTERPRISE DATA REPOSITORIES

From the 1990s onwards, companies assume that the value of data goes beyond transactions. Decision-making is becoming increasingly dependent on data analysis and business processes are consuming larger amounts of data, generated in different parts of the organisation and for different purposes. A trend is born that promotes the use of data for broader issues, which transcend the place where the transaction takes place. The need to create unique and integrated data warehouses becomes latent and projects of this type are considered and in some cases implemented. Data governance is gradually being identified as a fundamental practice for business success. At this stage initiatives are developed in a segmented way and around individual data silos and with a high degree of informality.

The data governance elements at this stage have the following characteristic:

Organization: Data authority generally exists in the IT spheres, however it has limited influence on business processes. Informally some business experts perform data management, yet there is no formalisation of this role or definition of responsibilities. IT understands that business involvement is fundamental to data. However, collaboration is often inconsistent and depends on the experts mentioned above.

Processes: There are defined processes around the integrated master data repositories of the company (individually on each of these). Data problems are dealt with in a reactive manner and without a systemic approach that goes to the root cause. IT has formal processes in place for making technical decisions about data. There are generally no institutionalised data processes in business areas.

Technology: There are integrated data warehouses and master data management systems of varying scope. IT invests in technologies for data quality and metadata management but only at the level of integrated data warehouses. Efforts to manage data across multiple systems are generally bottom-up and with limited influence.

3.2.2.1.4 STEP 3 - POLICY FOCUS

Despite efforts to consolidate and centralise business data, there is evidence of a parallel proliferation of departmental systems and data repositories dispersed across all levels and sectors of the organisation. This is due to the continued growth in the complexity and volume of data. Business use of data is becoming more sophisticated and this is driving new ways of manipulating, storing and presenting information. The strategic shifts that businesses take are taking over the medium and long term plans that are being executed and data needs cannot be solved by integrated data warehouses alone. Forward thinking companies recognise the problem and approach it in a different way. Internal data governance organisations are created to manage with formal processes the data set considered critical to results. The management focus was placed on data model policies, data quality, data security and data lifecycle management. Instead of focusing on data repositories, the focus is on implementing processes that define, apply and enforce data policies. Data repositories remain important, only now they are mounted on integrated data platforms and governed by a set of policies. There is a change in mentality that leads to greater business responsibility for data, which is valued as an asset. For IT this approach is liberating. Greater flexibility is obtained in the design of systems to cover the needs of the business, without giving up consistency and control.

The data governance elements at this stage have the following characteristic:

Organization: There is a central authority in the form of an interdisciplinary board and data managers are explicitly appointed and their responsibilities clearly specified. The company is dedicated to data management on a sustained basis. The mentality of data as one of the most important assets of the organisation is becoming established.
Processes: The processes for policy definition, communication and data application are implemented. A clear process is established for reporting and monitoring associated issues. Instead of having processes oriented to different data warehouses we have a single, simplified set of processes that govern the data and apply to all existing repositories.
Technology: A data policy repository is centrally managed to configure a set of data policies in a "top-down" way within the organization. Data governance processes are supported and managed with automated workflows. Data quality is regularly monitored and measured.

3.2.2.1.5 STAGE 4 - WIDELY REGULATED

This stage is characterised by the successful implementation of policy-focused data governance; there will be widespread and lasting improvements in business performance. Over time the scope of such programmes will be extended to cover all areas of data competence (Modelling, Safety, Quality and Life Cycle). The policies defined will reach all data assets considered of fundamental value by the business, the processes that produce and consume them and the information systems that store and manipulate them.
A work culture that values data as a strategic asset is installed and this is evident in all sectors of the business. Data governance becomes a permanent business function.
The data governance elements have the following characteristic:

Organization: The organisational structure for data governance becomes institutional for the company, which is given the same critical role as other business functions, such as human resources and finance for example. The business takes full responsibility for its data and the policies that govern it.
Processes: Data governance is a business process and decisions are made with quantifiable cost-benefit-risk analysis.
Technology: Business policies for the data model, data quality, security and lifecycle are integrated with user and data interaction. Centrally defined policies and rules shape the behaviour of systems where this is possible. Data at rest and data in flight are monitored. Data issues are proactively resolved before they adversely affect the business.

The Kalido model suggests self-assessment to enable companies to understand where they stand in terms of the governance of their data. This model provides a guide that facilitates the activity. We access this assessment through Kalido's data governance resource centre. This assessment was carried out considering the reality of the Asset, it was executed by the data manager and later sent to the specialists

of the company that owns the applied model; who returned the results and suggestions of the analysis carried out. For the purposes of this project, this analysis serves as a baseline of the current situation of the Asset in terms of data management.
The following are the results of the evaluation and the recommendations made by Kalido's consultants.

3.2.2.2 EVALUATION RESULTS

The results of the assessment will be presented taking into account the overall assessment of the maturity of the data governance model for Assets and also the assessment identified for each of the elements of the model. In our case the maturity values will range from one to four according to the stage we are at. To understand, see Table 3.

General graphic summary: In the graph shown in Figure 3 we can see the result of the evaluation carried out on the Santa Cruz Asset

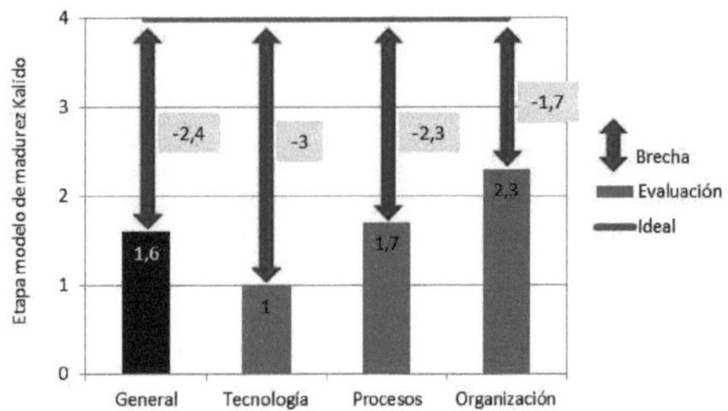

Figure 3: Chart of gaps between current and ideal scenario
Source: Adapted and translated from WINSTON, CHEN (2011). *Kalido Data Governance Maturity Assessment Report.* Information received by email.

The graph contains the result of the assessment and also shows the measured maturity for each element of the model. We attach to the evaluation result the existing gaps with the ideal model. In the case of the "Overall" result, this is obtained by averaging the assessments made for each element. In Table 8 you can see the detail of the results for each of the dimensions in the graph.

Table 8: Maturity assessment results of Data Governance activities for the Santa Cruz Assets

Dimensión	Etapa de madurez según evaluación Kalido
General	**Etapa 2: Centrado en los repositorios de datos de la Empresa,**
Organización	*Etapa 2: Centrado en los repositorios de datos de la Empresa,*
Procesos	*Etapa 2: Centrado en los repositorios de datos de la Empresa,*
Tecnología	*Etapa 1: Centrado en las aplicaciones TI,*

Note: Source: Adapted and translated from WINSTON, CHEN. (2011). *Kalido Data Governance Maturity Assessment Report.* Information received by email.

Below is a more detailed explanation of the results for each of the elements.

3.2.2.3 EXPLANATION OF RESULTS

Maturity of the ORGANIZATION component: The result indicates that the Santa Cruz Asset is in the stage; "*Focused on the Company's data repositories*". With an average value of (**2.3**). This indicates that the need to govern the data is recognized. However, this is exercised informally and roles are defined imprecisely, without a structural policy to support them. Collaboration between the IT area and the business on data issues is sporadic.

Maturity of the PROCESS component: The result indicates that the Santa Cruz Asset is in the stage; "*Focused on the Company's data repositories*". With an average value of (**1.7**). This result implies that the Asset has vaguely defined data governance processes, driven mostly by the implementation of enterprise and integrated data warehouses (ERP[9]). In the IT area there are formal procedures associated with the technical aspects of data management, there is not yet an integrated vision of the entire company, focused on the value of data as an asset to be managed as such.

Maturity of the TECHNOLOGY component: The result indicates that the Santa Cruz Asset is in the stage; "*Focused on IT applications*". With an average value of (**1**). This result indicates that in the technological aspects, data management is focused on the computer applications and transactions executed by this means. A large number of issues associated with data management fall to the IT area and their validation and handling is generally dependent on the specific application used in a given process. Typically this results in poor quality data, lack of multifunctional data view and poor understanding of how data is produced and consumed throughout the Asset.

3.2.2.4 EVALUATION DETAILS

In order to arrive at the above-mentioned results, a survey was carried out consisting of a series of questions grouped by each of the dimensions or elements of the maturity model used and at the same time classified according to the topic analyzed.
We will then present the groups of questions in the survey, which are focused on the elements of the model and the topic to be evaluated, and we will also identify the answers given by the Asset's referent.

A. **ORGANISATION: Evaluation details per topic. In this aspect the Asset achieved the value that represents the highest maturity with respect to the rest of the elements.**
AUTHORITY TOPIC:

In Table 9 we will see the different answer options for the question associated with "*Organization*" and for the topic "*Authority*". With a green background we highlight the answer selected by the Active Santa Cruz respondent. The last column of the table indicates the percentage of affirmative responses for each of the options presented for this question and according to the record of all surveys conducted by Kalido. The first column indicates the stage of maturity associated with the topic, according to the selection made. The original language in which the survey was conducted is maintained. This methodology is repeated for all the following topics.

Table 9: Question 1 and its different answers, according to the stage of maturity of the respondent

[9] Enterprise resource planning (ERP) systems integrate internal and external management of information across an entire organization-embracing finance/accounting, manufacturing, sales and service, customer relationship management, etc.

Q1 - Authority: Which group in your organization makes decisions for data across the enterprise?		
# Etapa de acuerdo respuesta	Opciones	% de respuestas afirmativas en evaluaciones de Kalido
1	No official authority for data; administrators for applications serve as the closest substitute.	39%
2	A formal group such as Data Architecture within IT has some control over data but lacks the necessary authority to change business processes.	33%
3	A council or board with high-level representation from some business functions. The council has the authority to change some business processes.	16%
4	A cross-organizational council or board with institutionalized, enterprise-wide authority for all key decisions involving data.	12%
		100%

Note: Source: Adapted and translated from WINSTON, CHEN. (2011). *Kalido Data Governance Maturity Assessment Report.*

DATA MANAGEMENT TOPIC (Table 10):

Table 10: Question 2 and its different answers, according to the stage of maturity of the respondent

Q2 - Data Stewarship: How well defined is the role of a Data Steward in your organization?		
# Etapa de acuerdo respuesta	Opciones	% de respuestas afirmativas en evaluaciones de Kalido
1	No data steward role. Traditional IT is the de facto steward of data.	30%
2	Informal data experts perform some of the tasks of stewardship, but their roles and responsibilities are not explicitly established.	49%
3	Formal data steward roles are defined and designated for some key data areas with clearly prescribed day-to-day activities.	17%
4	Data stewards are clearly designated for all key data areas. Stewards are highly visible focal points for data.	4%
		100%

Note: Source: Adapted and translated from WINSTON, CHEN. (2011). *Kalido Data Governance Maturity Assessment Report.*

TOPIC ROLE OF BUSINESS (Table 11):

Table 11: Question 3 and its different answers, according to the stage of maturity of the respondent

Q3 - Business Role: How engaged is the business in managing data and data policies?		
# Etapa de acuerdo respuesta	Opciones	% de respuestas afirmativas en evaluaciones de Kalido
1	Business has no clear role except to provide initial requirements for application development.	33%
2	Business fully participates in and sometimes leads projects, but its involvement is project-based rather than permanent.	47%
3	Business is engaged in a sustained way in managing data and data policies. Some end-to-end process owners take an active role in making data policies.	16%
4	Business takes full responsibility for data content and for data policy making.	4%
		100%

Note: Source: Adapted and translated from WINSTON, CHEN. (2011). *Kalido Data Governance Maturity Assessment Report.*

TOPIC COLLABORATION (Table 12):

Table 12: Question 4 and its different answers, according to the stage of maturity of the respondent

Q4 - Collaboration: What is the level of data collaboration between business and IT?		
# Etapa de acuerdo respuesta	Opciones	% de respuestas afirmativas en evaluaciones de Kalido
1	Rigid boundary exists between business and IT with little collaboration.	23%
2	Collaboration clearly exists. It is intense during a major initiative but is ad hoc on a day-to-day basis.	57%
3	Business-IT collaboration on data is institutionalized as a routine activity even in the absence of a major initiative.	14%
4	Business-IT collaboration related to data is pervasive throughout the enterprise.	6%
		100%

Note: Source: Adapted and translated from WINSTON, CHEN. (2011). *Kalido Data Governance Maturity Assessment Report.*

TOPIC RESPONSIBILITY (Table 13)

Table 13: Question 5 and its different answers, according to the stage of maturity of the respondent

Q5 - Accountability: Which group in your organization is accountable for data quality?		
# Etapa de acuerdo respuesta	Opciones	% de respuestas afirmativas en evaluaciones de Kalido
1	Traditional IT is completely accountable for data, but accountability is not aligned with business objectives.	28%
2	Traditional IT is accountable for data, and accountability is somewhat aligned with business objectives.	37%
3	Accountability for data and its quality is documented and assigned to the most appropriate individuals, typically not IT. However, there is typically no way to enforce accountability.	31%
4	Accountability for data is institutionalized with common, measurable performance metrics tied to employee performance.	4%
		100%

Note: Source: Adapted and translated from WINSTON, CHEN. (2011). *Kalido Data Governance Maturity Assessment Report.*

TOPICAL CULTURAL ATTITUDE (Table 14):

Table 14: Question 6 and its different answers, according to the stage of maturity of the respondent

Q6 - Cultural Attitude: Which of the following best describes your organization's view of data assets and their value?		
# Etapa de acuerdo respuesta	Opciones	% de respuestas afirmativas en evaluaciones de Kalido
1	Data is a by-product of business activities and not valued until someone needs it.	24%
2	Intuitive awareness that data is an asset, but the organization lacks a framework to determine the relative value of different types of data.	52%
3	The concept of data as an asset has emerged; data is valued, and activities are prioritized based on business impact.	21%
4	Pervasive culture of treating data as a strategic enterprise asset with quantifiable value.	3%
		100%

Note: Source: Adapted and translated from WINSTON, CHEN. (2011). *Kalido Data Governance Maturity Assessment Report.*

In Figure 4, we see a graphic summary in which we can see the gap between the current situation and the ideal maturity according to the model for "*Organisation"* and all its topics. It is important to say that the average of the stage number values obtained for each topic of the elements analysed is the final value of the topic.

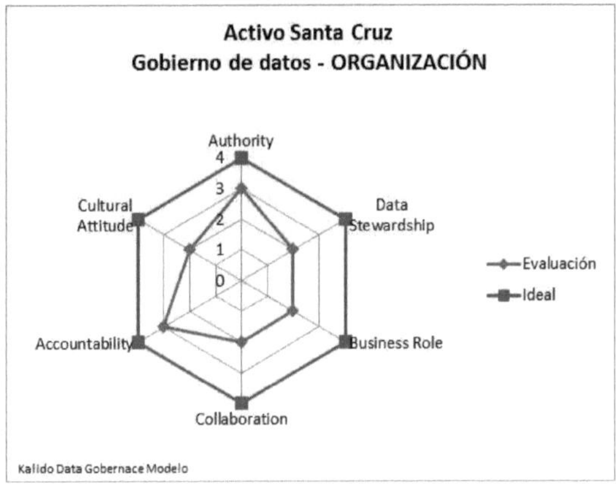

Figure 4: Gap chart for the analysis element ORGANISATION and its different topics; between current and ideal scenario.
Source: Generated on the basis of WINSTON, CHEN. (2011). *Kalido Data Governance Maturity Assessment Report.* Information received by email.

B. **PROCESS: Evaluation details per topic.**

POLICY MANAGEMENT TOPIC (Table 15): The evaluation criteria are the same as those used in the previous item.

Table 15: Question 1 and its different answers, according to the stage of maturity of the respondent

Q1 - Policy Management: What processes are in place for managing policies for data?		
# Etapa de acuerdo respuesta	Opciones	% de respuestas afirmativas en evaluaciones de Kalido
1	No concept of data policies. Rules for data are embedded in application logic and are not accessible.	26%
2	Loose and informal processes for data governance centered around major systems. The processes tend to degrade over time and are impossible to audit.	54%
3	Transparent processes for managing cross-system data policies are established. End-to-end process satisfies auditors and regulators.	16%
4	Data governance, including policy definition, implementation and enforcement is a core business process in its own right.	4%
		100%

Note: Source: Adapted and translated from WINSTON, CHEN. (2011). *Kalido Data Governance Maturity Assessment Report.*

COMMUNICATION TOPIC (Table 16):

Table 16: Question 2 and its different answers, according to the stage of maturity of the respondent

Q2 - Communication: How do you communicate decisions made about data and data policies?		
# Etapa de acuerdo respuesta	Opciones	% de respuestas afirmativas en evaluaciones de Kalido
1	Communication occurs during system deployment and training.	29%
2	Communication is infrequent and often in response to a crisis. It takes time and determination to discover policies.	51%
3	New and updated data policies are communicated to the people impacted; they are easily accessible when needed.	16%
4	Data policies pop up in context when applicable, and users are guided on how data should be created, used and handled.	4%
		100%

Note: Source: Adapted and translated from WINSTON, CHEN. (2011). *Kalido Data Governance Maturity Assessment Report.*

TOPIC MANAGEMENT OF DATA THEMES (Table 17):

Table 17: Question 3 and its different answers, according to the stage of maturity of the respondent

Q3 - Issue Resolution: What is the process for resolving data issues?		
# Etapa de acuerdo respuesta	Opciones	% de respuestas afirmativas en evaluaciones de Kalido
1	There is no way to raise data issues.	23%
2	An official channel for raising data issues exists but is not effective. Most problems are resolved through informal networks.	51%
3	Issues are recorded, reported and tracked through to resolution by data stewards working in collaboration with business and IT.	24%
4	Potential issues are identified in real time and remediated collaboratively before they can negatively impact the business.	2%
		100%

Note: Source: Adapted and translated from WINSTON, CHEN. (2011). *Kalido Data Governance Maturity Assessment Report.*

TOPIC OF DECISIONS (Table 18):

Table 18: Question 4 and its different answers, according to the stage of maturity of the respondent

Q4 - Decision Rights: What is the decision-making process for data?		
# Etapa de acuerdo respuesta	Opciones	% de respuestas afirmativas en evaluaciones de Kalido
1	Decisions for data are primarily made by IT.	23%
2	Decision-making is system specific and unstructured at the enterprise level.	63%
3	Decision-making is structured and decision rights are clearly defined and communicated.	10%
4	Decision-making for data is institutionalized and made with full understanding of the quantifiable benefit-cost-risk tradeoffs.	4%
		100%

Note: Source: Adapted and translated from WINSTON, CHEN. (2011). *Kalido Data Governance Maturity Assessment Report.*

<u>TOPIC PERFORMANCE (Table 19)</u>:

Table 19: Question 5 and its different answers, according to the stage of maturity of the respondent

Q5 - Performance Management: How do you measure the performance of data management activities?		
# Etapa de acuerdo respuesta	Opciones	% de respuestas afirmativas en evaluaciones de Kalido
1	No performance management.	54%
2	Metrics are system specific and heavily IT operations oriented.	27%
3	Some operational metrics for data governance program have been established and are tracked. They are tied to business needs.	14%
4	Key metrics on efficiency and effectiveness are standardized. Actuals and goals are compared for variance.	5%
		100%

Note: Source: Adapted and translated from WINSTON, CHEN. (2011). *Kalido Data Governance Maturity Assessment Report.*

<u>TOPIC DATA FLOWS (Table 20)</u>:

Table 20: Question 6 and its different answers, according to the stage of maturity of the respondent

Q6 - Dataflow Transparency: How transparent and accessible are the data flows among your systems and business processes?		
# Etapa de acuerdo respuesta	Opciones	% de respuestas afirmativas en evaluaciones de Kalido
1	Data authors do not know who will use the data or how the data will be used. Data consumers do not know where the data comes from.	26%
2	IT has some documentation on dataflows from authors to consumers, but business in general does not.	48%
3	Dataflows for some core processes are documented and accessible by data authors and consumers so that they're aware of the dependencies.	22%
4	Full transparency of how key enterprise data assets are produced and consumed. Data's downstream impact is well understood.	4%
		100%

Note: Source: Adapted and translated from WINSTON, CHEN. (2011). *Kalido Data Governance Maturity Assessment Report.*

In Figure 5, we see a graphic summary in which we can appreciate the gap between the current situation and the ideal maturity according to the model for "*<u>Processes</u>*" and all its topics.

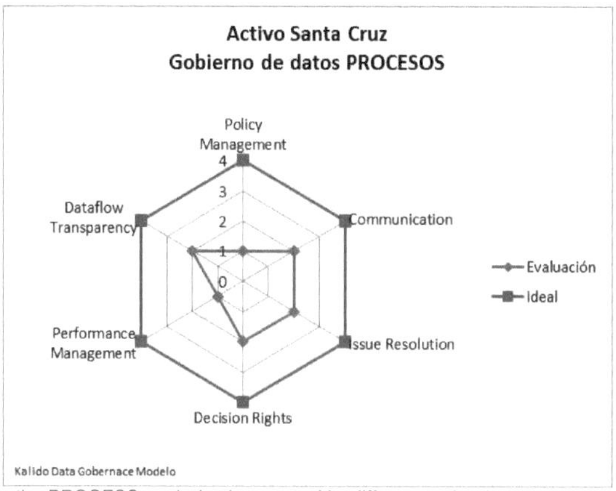

Figure 5: Gap chart for the PROCESS analysis element and its different topics; between current and ideal scenario. Source: Generated on the basis of WINSTON, CHEN. (2011). *Kalido Data Governance Maturity Assessment Report.* Information received by email.

A. **TECHNOLOGY: Evaluation details per topic. Here we got the lowest value. It is the one with the greatest opportunity for improvement.**

TOPIC RULES AND DATA POLICIES (Table 21): The evaluation criteria are the same as those used above.

Table 21: Question 1 and its different answers, according to the stage of maturity of the respondent

Q1 - Data Policies and Rules: Where are data policies and rules stored?		
# Etapa de acuerdo respuesta	**Opciones**	**% de respuestas afirmativas en evaluaciones de Kalido**
1	No concept of data policies. Rules for data are embedded in application logic and not accessible.	31%
2	Policies and rules exist in loosely documented form. They are not managed through a central and easily accessible repository.	53%
3	Common enterprise repository of data quality policies and rules established, accessible by all stakeholders including business and IT.	14%
4	Common and pervasive policy layer for data quality, security and lifecycle fully integrated with key systems.	2%
		100%

Note: Source: Adapted and translated from WINSTON, CHEN. (2011). *Kalido Data Governance Maturity Assessment Report.*

PROCESS DEPLOYMENT TOPIC (Table 22):

Table 22: Question 2 and its different answers, according to the stage of maturity of the respondent

Q2 - Process Orchestration: How does technology support the process of data governance in your organization?		
# Etapa de acuerdo respuesta	Opciones	% de respuestas afirmativas en evaluaciones de Kalido
1	No data governance process exists to be supported.	43%
2	Informal workflow using office desktop application and general purpose collaboration tools such as SharePoint.	46%
3	Data governance processes are orchestrated by workflow with automation to guide the day-to-day activities of the extended data organization.	9%
4	Data governance processes are orchestrated by workflow and integrated with enterprise workflow engine.	2%
		100%

Note: Source: Adapted and translated from WINSTON, CHEN. (2011). *Kalido Data Governance Maturity Assessment Report.*

COMPLIANCE MANAGEMENT TOPIC (Table 23):

Table 23: Question 3 and its different answers, according to the stage of maturity of the respondent

Q3 - Compliance Monitoring: What mechanisms are deployed for monitoring compliance to data policies and rules?		
# Etapa de acuerdo respuesta	Opciones	% de respuestas afirmativas en evaluaciones de Kalido
1	Data consumers discover data issues during the course of use but don't know who to inform for correction.	42%
2	IT uses tool-specific features (for example ETL rejection) to detect violations to rules. Data consumers don't have a way to report additional data issues.	47%
3	Active monitoring is deployed and run regularly on multiple data repositories to assess compliance. Data consumers can easily raise issues.	8%
4	Data quality and security monitoring against policies in place for all key data elements and run on both stored and in-flight data. Data consumers have in-system ways of alerting data stewards of errors.	3%
		100%

Note: Source: Adapted and translated from WINSTON, CHEN. (2011). *Kalido Data Governance Maturity Assessment Report.*

MODELED TOPIC (Table 24):

Table 24: Question 4 and its different answers, according to the stage of maturity of the respondent

Q4 - Modeling: What type of modeling does your organization perform for data, systems and business processes?		
# Etapa de acuerdo respuesta	Opciones	% de respuestas afirmativas en evaluaciones de Kalido
1	Models exist for each application only.	49%
2	IT produces bottoms-up, inventory-style metadata management that lacks business visibility and control. Top-down models are not actively used.	37%
3	Unified and business-accessible models for data, business processes and systems strongly influence system development.	10%
4	Top-down model actively drives the design and behavior of key systems.	4%
		100%

Note: Source: Adapted and translated from WINSTON, CHEN. (2011). *Kalido Data Governance Maturity Assessment Report.*

CRITICAL DATA MANAGEMENT TOPIC (Table 25):

Table 25: Question 5 and its different answers, according to the stage of maturity of the respondent

Q5 - Master Data Management: How does your organization manage master data?		
# Etapa de acuerdo respuesta	Opciones	% de respuestas afirmativas en evaluaciones de Kalido
1	Master data resides in disparate applications and is unmanaged.	49%
2	Single or multi-domain MDM (typically for customer or product master data) is implemented but lacks governance.	39%
3	Multiple MDM platforms work in concert with a central data governance application to implement and execute enterprise data policies for master data.	8%
4	Master data complies with enterprise data policies and rules at the points of origin.	4%
		100%

Note: Source: Adapted and translated from WINSTON, CHEN. (2011). *Kalido Data Governance Maturity Assessment Report.*

DATA QUALITY TOPIC (Table 26):

Table 26: Question 6 and its different answers, according to the stage of maturity of the respondent

Q6 - Data Quality: How is data quality measured by your organization?		
# Etapa de acuerdo respuesta	Opciones	% de respuestas afirmativas en evaluaciones de Kalido
1	Data quality is poor and is not measured.	48%
2	IT runs data profiling and cleansing in an ad hoc manner and on narrow uses cases at the repository level.	36%
3	Data quality for key data assets is measured holistically, reported and tracked over time to sustainably improve it.	12%
4	Data quality metrics are pervasive and presented in context to help consumers use data effectively.	4%
		100%

Note: Source: Adapted and translated from WINSTON, CHEN. (2011). *Kalido Data Governance Maturity Assessment Report.*

In Figure 6, we see a graphic summary in which we can appreciate the gap between the current situation and the ideal maturity according to the model for the *Technology* component and all its topics.

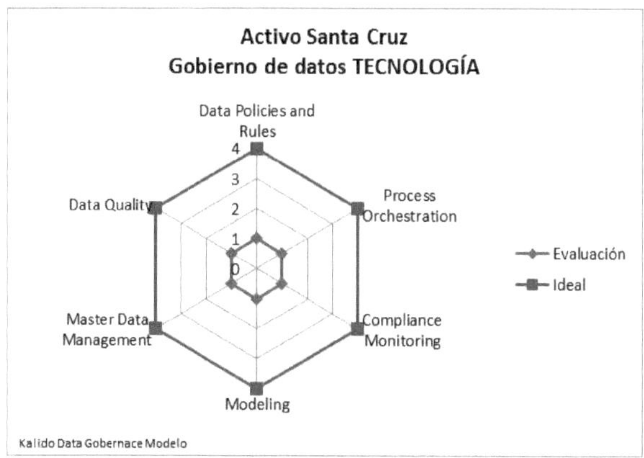

Figure 6: Gap chart for the analysis element TECHNOLOGY and its different topics; between current and ideal scenario.

Source: Generated on the basis of WINSTON, CHEN. (2011). *Kalido Data Governance Maturity Assessment Report.* Information received by email.

All of the above is intended to reflect the current state of data governance practices. We establish the starting point of the project. While the evaluation we have just presented applies to all data management processes involved in the development of Asset activities, the scope of this project aims to focus on the processes set out in point 2.2 of this document.

3.2.2.5 HISTORICAL BACKGROUND

In order to get into the historical background of the issues that our project is trying to solve, we will first mention those associated with the recent history of the company. Then we will mention general background of other organizations in the country and the region that participate in the same market segment.

3.2.2.5.1 FOCUS ON PETROLERA DEL SUR AND ACTIVO SANTA CRUZ

There are a number of precedents that demonstrate the growing interest that data management has taken in the company. Sometimes the subject is addressed by specific projects in which new information management technologies are applied, in others; the interest arises from the need to optimise decision-making processes and interdisciplinary collaboration.

The greatest progress was made between 2008 and 2009, when a specific data governance process was defined for the "*Oil or Gas Exploration and Production*" area, and progress was also made in defining the role of data manager within this same area. In the last months of 2009, the company made decisions on organisational restructuring. This generated changes that had a negative impact on all the projected and ongoing initiatives related to this issue. Only a few data managers were appointed, all of them located within the E&P area. Unfortunately, the restructuring did not allow the process to be consolidated, the defined data governance process was not applied and the organisation of the appointed data managers was not organised with the necessary formality and scope.

In 2008, after a comprehensive evaluation of the project, a business case was generated with an associated project, in which one of the solution elements was the implementation of a data management system. [8]. The 2009 restructuring had a negative impact on the project and it was not approved. Nevertheless, from 2008 onwards, different initiatives have been implemented that allowed for a more conscious consideration of the importance of considering data and information as an important element, which must be managed. The need to start generating specific initiatives is identified within the formal areas of discussion. The first difficulty that arises is that of being able to justify, from the point of view of benefits, the investment in this type of project. So, research was carried out to find out *how the* leading organisations and references in these areas tackled the problem. This is how we arrived at DAMA and the whole body of knowledge that this organisation managed to formalise after years of work and research. We also studied numerous success cases, analysed diverse documentation associated with the subject and considered different management and evaluation models to apply (See section 4 of the bibliography and resources). With all this and the experience gathered by the Asset and the company to date, we obtained the foundations that led us to define the execution of a pilot project with a well-defined scope and impact on the results.

An important aspect to highlight in this section, is that in the operational model of Petrolera del Sur and Activo Santa Cruz, labour is hired from service companies, this reaches more than 90% of the personnel associated to the operations. This indicates that most of the data generated and acquired in the work processes are the responsibility of personnel external to the Company. It is also known that in current service contracts there is not always a special section specifying aspects related to data and the degree of responsibility that exists over these, in cases where requirements are specified; the view is limited only to the needs of customers of the process involved or to some current regulations that must be complied with. The project aims to address and adjust this problem and at the same time seeks to obtain benefits from it. This aspect is specified in more detail in the following sections of the document.

3.2.2.5.2 FOCUS ON OTHER ORGANIZATIONS IN THE REGION AND COUNTRY

When we investigated the state of affairs of the organisations in the segment, we were able to determine that the experience in terms of data management and governance is similar to that of Petrolera del Sur. This is consistent with various assessments made at an international level, which estimated that by 2012 in terms of governance and data quality, less than 10% of organisations will have a high level of maturity (Stage 3 or 4 of the Kalido model)[10].

In most companies there is a latent interest in managing their data and information efficiently. In some cases, activities associated with specific data problems are developed (Compliance with regulations, implementation of control panels, data quality projects, etc.) and in others the interest is associated with the application of new information technologies that facilitate or allow for improved management. We observe that there is still a lack of organisation and alignment of resources and management elements to consider data as a valuable asset. The focus and objective of the initiatives are more oriented towards the improvement of processes and the incorporation of new information technologies. The application of specific practices aimed at establishing a data strategy with an integrated vision has not yet been identified. There were also activities promoted by organisations which bring together companies in the sector (IAPG[11], PPDM[12], etc.) which aim to encourage the generation of spaces for collaboration and discussion in which they can share their experience in this area.

It was also identified that the most frequent triggers for addressing initiatives associated with data management and governance relate to the following aspects:

- **Compliance with current regulations**: Laws such as Sarbanes & Oxley or[13] others of a national nature oblige organisations in the sector to comply with specific requirements in terms of the ways of presenting and/or treating the information achieved. Compliance or non-compliance with these regulations can have a significant impact on business results.
- **Improvements in geographic data management**: The rise of new technologies that facilitate the management of geographic information, its visual analysis through interactive maps has forced companies in the sector to manage this type of data with appropriate standards.
- **Application of ERP[14]technologies** : This type of project forces organizations to consider aspects of data managed by the technology to be implemented. Most companies in the sector have developed projects of this type.

As for the evolution of results for companies in the sector in the region, the scenario is also similar. Costs rise and production declines. In the specific case of our country this is accentuated, aggravated by the fall in investment levels.

3.2.3 STUDY OF THE SITUATION TO BE ACHIEVED

Earlier we clearly described the gap between the current scenario and the target in terms of data governance. The characterisation of the current scenario and the target is specified in a consolidated and schematic way in Table 27. It considers the evaluation made according to the criteria of the model applied and shows us for each element and topic of the model the characteristics of the current and expected maturity at the end of the project. [15].

3.2.3.1 IMPACT ON THE PROCESSES ACHIEVED

The processes involved in the project are:

- **Production monitoring and control process.**

---

[10] NASCIO Staff. (03 of 2009). Data Governance Part II: Maturity Models - A Path to Progress. Retrieved 05 May 2013, from NASCIO: http://www.nascio.org/publications/documents/NASCIO-DataGovernancePTII.pdf

[11] IAPG: Argentine Institute of Oil and Gas.

[12] PPDM: Professional Petroleum Data Management Association

[13] SARBANES & OXLEY Act enacted in the U.S. Congress following the financial frauds carried out by ENRON and other major U.S. companies The law aims to achieve greater transparency in terms of the information that companies disclose about their financial results. The law applies to all companies listed on the New York Stock Exchange.

[14] Enterprise resource planning (ERP) systems are management information systems that integrate and manage many of the businesses associated with the production operations and distribution aspects of a company's production of goods or services.

Within this project it is expected to improve the aspects related to data collection, considering the opportunity, the use and the quality of the data. To this end, the evaluation carried out will be considered in the first instance. The process will be analysed in detail, considering the data as an important resource to be managed and the necessary effort will be made to design and apply a strategy to align all the elements involved. Metrics applied to this process will be defined to allow us to decide on its evolution. The aspects of the process that are expected to have an impact are

- Review and redefine the roles and functions involved, seeking to clearly establish the limits of responsibility for the data.
- Greater integration between the systems involved in data management.
- Improve the quality of the data at the time it originates.
- Reduce the time spent by people handling and transforming data.
- Make the systems providers of data and information structured and according to the needs of the different clients of the process.
- Determine the costs of acquiring and maintaining data handled by the process.
- Adapt service contracts and align them with the data strategy defined for the process.

Table 27: Data Governance Gap to be addressed by the project

	Elemento del modelo	Tópico evaluado	Situación actual	Situación objetivo Etapa 4: "Ampliamente regulados"
Modelo Kalido "MADUREZ en GOBIERNO DE DATOS"	Organización Etapa actual (2): "Centrado en los repositorios de datos de la Empresa"	Autoridad	Existe un comité con representantes de alto nivel de algunas funciones de la empresa. El Consejo tiene la autoridad para cambiar algunos de los procesos del negocio.	Un grupo formal (institucionalizado) y conformado por personal del negocio y de TI existe y tiene la autoridad suficiente para tomar decisiones sobre temas de datos para los procesos del negocio que estén dentro de su alcance.
		Administración de datos	Expertos en el manejo de datos del negocio existen informalmente y realizan algunas de las tareas de administración, pero sus funciones y responsabilidades no se han establecido de forma clara y explícita.	Los administradores de datos están claramente designados para los procesos alcanzados. Sus funciones y responsabilidades están formalizadas.
		Reglas de negocio	Los expertos de datos del negocios participan activamente y en ocasiones conducen proyectos, pero su participación se basa en proyectos y no permanente.	Mediante los administradores de datos el negocio asume plena responsabilidad por el contenido de los datos y la elaboración de políticas de datos.
		Colaboración	La colaboración existe en temas de datos. Es intensa cuando hay vigentes iniciativas importantes, pero es a demanda en el día a día.	La colaboración entre el negocio y TI en temas de datos es una práctica generalizada.
		Responsabilidad	La responsabilidad sobre los datos y su calidad se documenta para los procesos críticos del negocio y se asigna a las personas más adecuadas, por lo general no son de TI. Sin embargo, no existe aún una forma de distribuir la responsabilidad a lo largo y ancho de la organización.	La responsabilidad sobre los datos se institucionaliza con métricas de rendimiento medibles ligados al desempeño de los empleados directos e indirectos (Especificaciones de Contrato).
		Actitud cultural	Existe conciencia intuitiva sobre la importancia y el valor de los datos, pero la organización carece de un marco para determinar el valor relativo de los mismos.	Para los procesos del negocio alcanzados por el proyecto existe una cultura generalizada del tratamiento de los datos como un activo estratégico de la empresa y con un valor cuantificable.
	Procesos Etapa actual (2): "Centrado en los repositorios de datos de la Empresa"	Gestión de políticas	No existe un concepto claro de políticas de datos. Las reglas para los datos se insertan en la lógica de las aplicaciones de gestión de datos involucradas y no siempre son accesibles.	Los datos son gobernados. Se incluyen políticas de datos formales y aplicadas sobre los procesos del negocio (Independientemente de las aplicaciones que intervienen). Esta es una decisión del negocio que reconoce la importancia de aplicarlas y asegurar su cumplimiento.
		Comunicación	La comunicación de temas de datos es poco frecuente y, a menudo en respuesta a una crisis. Se necesita tiempo y determinación para descubrir las políticas necesarias (Gestión reactiva).	Las políticas de datos surgen en el contexto de aplicación de los mismos (Considera el origen), y los usuarios son informados y guiados sobre cómo crear, utilizar y manipular los datos.
		Resolución de temas de datos	Existe un canal oficial para plantear cuestiones de datos, este no es eficaz. La mayoría de los problemas se resuelven a través de redes informales.	Los problemas potenciales de datos se identifican en tiempo real y en colaboración con TI, estos son remediados antes de que puedan influir negativamente en el negocio.
		Toma de decisiones	La toma de decisiones en cuanto a datos es específica del sistema involucrado y no estructurados e integrados a nivel de empresa.	La toma de decisiones sobre el tema de datos se institucionaliza y se consideran aspectos de costo-beneficio y minimización de los riesgos con un punto de vista integral de la empresa.
		Performance	No existen métricas formales en cuanto a desempeño en el manejo de datos. Solo se miden aspectos específicos que permiten minimizar riesgos y mejorar aspectos de gestión.	Para los procesos alcanzados existen métricas clave para medir la eficiencia y la eficacia en cuanto a la gestión de los datos. Valores reales y las metas se comparan por su variación.
		Flujo de datos	En TI existe documentación dispersa sobre flujos de datos, pero en el negocio por lo general no es así.	Para los procesos alcanzados existe documentación formal de como los activos de datos se producen y se consumen. Los mismos se entienden y conocen por todos los actores que intervienen y también consideran todo el ciclo de vida del dato.
	Tecnología Etapa actual (1): "Centrado en las aplicaciones TI"	Reglas y políticas de datos	No existe aún un claro concepto de políticas de datos. Las reglas existentes para los datos están embebidas en la lógica de las aplicaciones por medio de las cuales se manipulan y estas no son fácilmente accesibles por los referentes del negocio.	Existe para los procesos alcanzados, políticas de calidad de datos que abarcan todos los sistemas claves involucrados y consideran el ciclo de vida completo de los datos y su seguridad. Las mismas se encuentran integradas con los sistemas.
		Despliegue de procesos	No existen procesos formales de gobierno de datos.	Los procesos de gobierno de datos están desplegados con los flujos de trabajo y se integran con la estrategia empresarial.
		Gestión de cumplimiento	Los consumidores de datos descubren problemas de datos en el curso de su uso, pero no siempre tienen claro a quién informar para su corrección y tampoco el impacto que significa no hacerlo.	Existe un control de calidad y seguridad para los datos claves de los procesos. Los mismos se realizan sobre los datos almacenados y al vuelo en origen de los mismos. Los consumidores de datos saben y tienen herramientas de notificación a los administradores de datos cuando encuentran errores de datos.
		Modelado	El modelado de datos existe dentro del alcance de cada aplicación que interviene en el manejo de los datos.	Existe un modelo de arriba hacia abajo que impulsa e integra activamente el diseño y comportamiento de los modelos embebidos con los sistemas claves involucrados.
		Gestión de datos críticos	Los datos críticos residen en aplicaciones dispersas y no siempre son administrados con visión integrada y con el rigor que corresponde.	La administración de los datos críticos cumple con las políticas y las reglas de datos empresariales definidas y las mismas se aplican desde los puntos de origen de los mismos.
		Calidad de datos	Por lo general los consumidores de datos perciben que la calidad de los datos no es adecuada y no se mide.	Existen y se aplican métricas de calidad de datos de forma generalizada para los procesos involucrados. Estas se presentan en el contexto para ayudar a los consumidores que utilizan los datos.

Note: Source: Generated and adapted based on WINSTON, CHEN. (2011). Kalido Data Governance Maturity Assessment Report. Information received by email.

➢ **Process of diffusion and dissemination of the production.**

It is critical for the activities of Activo Santa Cruz and Petrolera del Sur to comply with all production dissemination and disclosure requirements. Considering both internal and external clients. In this sense, the project aims to reduce to zero the risk of non-compliance with any requirement associated with the communication of the Asset's production that could impact on business results (Fines, Warnings, Quality of the data disseminated, Regulations and deadlines for communication of production, etc.))
The main impact of the project on this process will be on the risk associated with non-compliance. We will seek to maximise the use of technology and people skills to generate transparent processes for proactive management of data issues.

➢ **Process of determining and monitoring the causes of production losses.**

Historically, Petrolera del Sur has detected opportunities for improvement in the way it determines and manages production losses. We can say that this process is a sub process of the process of monitoring and controlling production. We will treat it separately since the impact on this process is what justifies the economic benefits of the project. As with the process of monitoring and controlling production, this process will take into account the evaluation carried out and will also seek to have a favourable impact on the activities of obtaining, appropriateness and use of the data. The following aspects of the process itself are expected to be improved:

- Review and redefine the criteria for classifying production losses. Align them with the production strategy of the Asset and the company.
- Properly classify losses at the point of origin.
- To facilitate and improve the processes of obtaining data and information on production losses.
- Facilitate integration processes between applications.
- Favour the reduction of the impact of gas production losses on potential gas production to **7% and** a consequent increase of **2% in** output.
- Favour the reduction of the impact of oil and petrol production losses on the potential production of these products to **9% and** a consequent increase of **24%** in production.

➢ **Process of monitoring and controlling the costs associated with production.**

On the Assets side, the evolution of expenses over the last five years has increased by more than fifty percent. Within the operational strategy of the Assets there are objectives associated with the identification of opportunities to improve their performance. In line with this, the project hopes to promote improvements in the following aspects of management and decision-making:

- Improve integration between operational and financial data management applications.
- Facilitate the timely collection of useful information in the spaces of critical analysis of the costs executed.
- Disseminate the importance of complying with the classification criteria of expenses when allocating them.
- To reduce the time of classification and obtaining critical data for the analysis of expenses.

The project includes the definition of all the necessary and appropriate metrics to measure the impact on each of the processes.

3.3 TECHNICAL ASPECTS OF THE PROJECT

3.3.1 THE SIZE AND LOCATION OF THE PROJECT

This project has a limited scope in the critical processes of the Santa Cruz Asset (Critical means the processes that have a direct impact on the business results and at the same time fall under the responsibility of the Asset). It is given the character of Pilot since the evaluation of its result is expected to promote the definition of a strategy that allows the promotion of new projects associated with data management, with a greater scope within the company and considering this experience.

3.3.2 BASIC STUDIES

3.3.2.1 FEASIBILITY

The following aspects were considered to determine the feasibility of the project:

- Within the Asset, an analysis of the current scenario and the activities that should be developed to achieve the expected results was carried out (See Schedule in section [**6.1**]). The following conclusions can be drawn from the analysis:
    - There is a relationship between the reduction of production losses and the development of data management initiatives. See Figures 14 and 15 in section [**5.5.2**]. This is the first indication of the feasibility of achieving benefits with this project.
    - The percentage impact of losses on sales was applied to the gas sales projection of the Asset for the periods that the project will last, without considering the 2 percentage point decrease proposed by the project for periods 3 and 4. The same was then done by applying the two-point decrease for the aforementioned periods[15]. The two percentage point decrease in gas losses was determined by considering the current trend and verifying that through a better classification of the loss cause data would allow the operation to have better information to make better decisions to achieve the objective. Between 2008 and 2012, a decrease of 7 percentage points was achieved.
    - The same analysis seen in the previous item was made for the sale of oil + petrol. In this case a reduction of the impact of the losses of these products by 3 percentage points[16]was considered. The improvement would also lie in a better classification of the causes of losses. Although in this case we do not have objective indications that allow us to infer the feasibility, if we could verify a deficient classification of the causes of losses and the operating personnel of the asset and the high management consider it feasible to achieve this objective as a[17]minimum .
    - The feasibility of including specific aspects related to data acquisition and registration in the Asset's contracts with the various service companies was verified. This aspect is fundamental given that the data associated with the processes achieved by the project are mostly generated and manipulated by third parties. It will be necessary to align the data strategy with the contracts.
    - Shortcomings were identified in the processes of classifying production-related costs. This generates inefficiencies when analyzing the data and identifying deviations between what was executed and what was planned. The feasibility of introducing improvements from the project was determined, which will make the process more efficient. The objective is to gain time in the analysis and reduce the time spent on verifying and correcting the data. The benefits of the project do not include improvements derived from this optimisation. If you consider measuring them for future projects of greater scope.

---

[15] The information in this analysis is not included due to the possibility of its dissemination to the Organization.

[16] The information in this analysis is not included due to the possibility of its dissemination to the Organization.

[17] The information in this analysis is not included due to the possibility of its dissemination to the Organization.

- The feasibility of having external consultants willing to work in Argentina and in the city of Rio Gallegos was verified.

- It was considered a volume of investment that has an appropriate dimension and that can be managed by the Asset.
- Through meetings with the right level of decision-makers, the details of the initiative were explained and the impact of implementing it was conveyed. The necessary political support was obtained for the preparation and presentation of the project profile to the Company's Project Evaluation Committee for the E&P area.

These aspects, considered critical to evaluate the feasibility of the project, allowed us to ensure its viability.

3.3.2.2 CONCEPTUAL MODEL

This project is based on the concepts and framework developed in DAMA's body of knowledge. In summary, *it raises the need to accept data management as an emerging discipline that promotes the processing of data and information as a resource, just as human or financial resources are. From this approach, it determines that data has a life cycle and this must be managed, without ceasing to consider the planning and specification of these, even before they are created or acquired. The model also highlights that data management must be considered a strategic function within the business, oriented to the planning, control and development of data resources. It considers the activity as a shared responsibility between IT professionals and data managers/administrators who must represent the collective interests of all data producers and consumers in the different areas of the company* [1].
To describe the scope of the discipline, the model proposes a decomposition of the discipline into ten management functions. These functions are:

I. **Data governance**: Plan, monitor and control the management of data and its use
II. **Data architecture management**: Define the model for managing data resources.
III. **Data development**: Analyze, design, implement, control and maintain data solutions according to business needs.
IV. **Operational data management**: Develop, maintain and support structured business data.
V. **Data security management**: Ensure privacy, confidentiality and appropriate access to data.
VI. **Reference and master data management**: Manage references of business critical data. Ensure consistent use of data across different business processes
VII. **Data Warehouse Management and Business Intelligence**: Develop solutions for information output and analysis needs.
VIII. **Document and content management**: Manage data and information that is outside the databases.
IX. **Management of metadata**: Integrate, control and provide management of data data.
X. **Data quality management**: Define, monitor and improve data quality.

In Figure 7 we can see a diagram representing the proposed functions. The model, clearly; raises the function of "*Data Governance*" as the heart of the model. To each of the proposed functions the model adds a set of context variables that allow us to characterize the current situation in an organization and then follow its evolution. The elements or environment variables proposed by DAMA are those represented in Figure 8.
In Figure 9 we can see a matrix that relates the functional aspects (Functions) with the context variables proposed by the model (Environment).
For each function the proposed framework offers a series of activities classified as

- **Planning activities (P)**: Activities that set the strategic and tactical course for other data management activities.
- **Control activities (C)**: Control activities associated with a specific function that is executed continuously.

- **Development activities (D)**: Activities carried out within the framework of the projects associated with the data strategy
- **Operational activities (O)**: Service activities and continuous support to business operations.

Figure 7: DAMA's proposed data management function group
Fuente: MOSLEY, M., BRACKETT, M., EARLEY, S. y HENDERSON, D. (2009). *The DAMA Guide to The Data Management Body of Knowledge (DAMA-DMBOOK Guide).* NJ 07720 U.S.A. Technics Publications, LLC.

The model maintains that the proposed guide is applicable to any type of organizational environment and that the bases and foundations of the model are the result of more than 50 years of work since the emergence of the first multidisciplinary groups dedicated to research and development of Data and Information Management practices, to date.

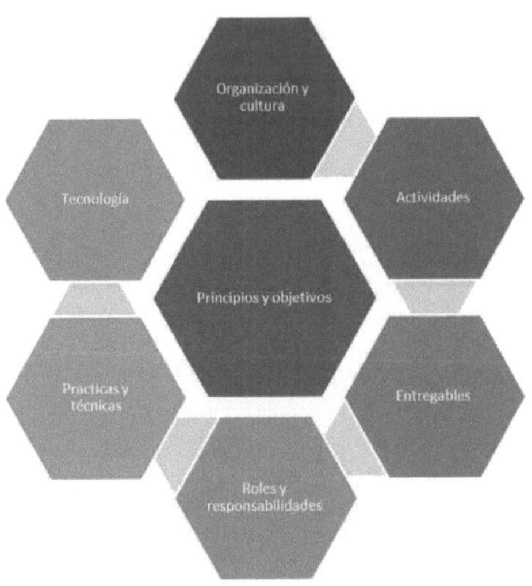

Figure 8: Environment variables to be considered for each data management function
Fuente: MOSLEY, M., BRACKETT, M., EARLEY, S. y HENDERSON, D. (2009). *The DAMA Guide to The Data Management Body of Knowledge (DAMA-DMBOOK Guide).* NJ 07720 U.S.A. Technics Publications, LLC.

	Variables de contexto						
Funciones - Gestión de datos	Principios y objetivos	Organización y cultura	Actividades	Entregables	Roles y responsabilidades	Practicas y técnicas	Tecnología
Gobierno de datos							
Gestión de arquitectura de datos							
Desarrollo de datos							
Gestión de datos operacionales							
Gestión de seguridad de datos							
Gestión de referencias y datos maestros							
Gestión de almacén de datos e Inteligencia de negocios							
Gestión de documentos y contenidos							
Gestión de meta datos							
Gestión de la calidad de los datos							

Figure 9: Matrix linking data management functions to context variables
Fuente: MOSLEY, M., BRACKETT, M., EARLEY, S. y HENDERSON, D. (2009). *The DAMA Guide to The Data Management Body of Knowledge (DAMA-DMBOOK Guide).* NJ 07720 U.S.A. Technics Publications, LLC.

To finish summarizing the generalities of what DAMA proposes, we present in Figure 10 a context diagram that defines the discipline and gives us greater clarity about its organization.

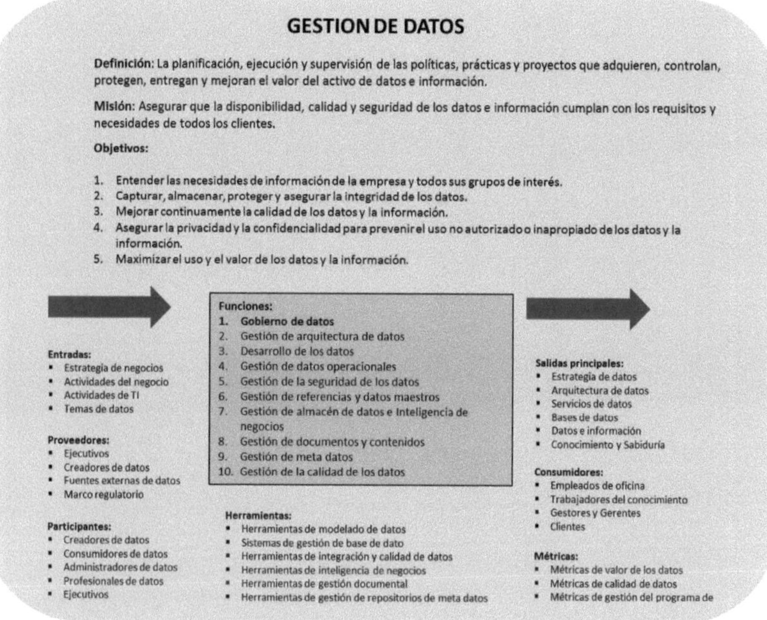

Figure 10: Conceptual scheme of data management
Fuente: MOSLEY, M., BRACKETT, M., EARLEY, S. y HENDERSON, D. (2009). *The DAMA Guide to The Data Management Body of Knowledge (DAMA-DMBOOK Guide).* NJ 07720 U.S.A. Technics Publications, LLC.

As we saw earlier, the framework proposed by DAMA sets out the "*Cat Government*" as the main function within its constituent function group. It is no accident that our project is based on the design of a data governance system that applies to critical Asset processes. In Figure 11 we can see a context diagram that defines the function according to DAMA. In this diagram we see that two types of activity are grouped together, these are "Data Management Planning" and "Data Management Control", defined as planning and control tasks respectively and assuming the concepts of activity type described above.

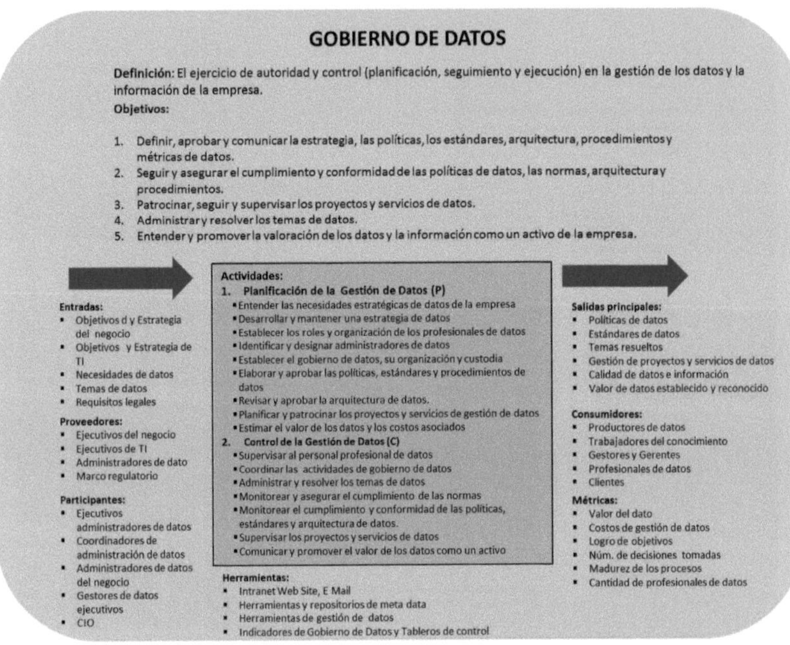

Figure 11: Conceptual scheme of data governance
Fuente: MOSLEY, M., BRACKETT, M., EARLEY, S. y HENDERSON, D. (2009). *The DAMA Guide to The Data Management Body of Knowledge (DAMA-DMBOOK Guide).* NJ 07720 U.S.A. Technics Publications, LLC.

The entire project development phase will be based on these concepts and they will be complemented with external support, specific training and with tools already known and applied by the company in other similar initiatives.

3.3.3 THE NECESSARY TECHNICAL PROCESSES

In addition to the concepts set out in the previous section, the project will use the following techniques and tools

I. **Kalido Model**: This methodology will be applied to measure the maturity of the data governance programme implemented on the processes achieved.
II. **Techniques and methodologies for process and workflow surveys**: We will use those known and managed by the IT area for similar projects.
III. **BPM and BPMN**: Business Process Management and Business Process Model Notation (set of symbols and graphics under standard that facilitate the modeling of business processes). In both cases, the tools and methods proposed by the Process Analyst of the IT area will be used. As an example we can see in sections [**6.2 Annex II**] and [**6.3 Annex III**]: Process map diagrammed with these techniques and RECI[18] Matrix that complements it respectively.

---

[18] **RECI Matrix**: This is a double-entry table that relates the activities and actors involved in a process. For each activity, it determines the function or degree of participation of the actors, classifying them as **Responsible for the** activity, **Execute** the activity, **Control the activity** or Be **informed** about the activity.

IV. **Survey techniques**: Observation of formal and informal documentation of the processes achieved. Working meetings under the modality of "Workshop" with personnel referring to them. Field visits, surveys, interviews, etc.
V. **Techniques and methodologies acquired in the training of resources**: New techniques and tools acquired in the training and certification process.
VI. **Techniques and methodologies proposed by the external consultancy**.
VII. **Documentary and dissemination techniques and methodologies**: Those applied in the company's communications model will be considered and other alternatives will be evaluated in the event that those in force are considered not to apply or are not effective for the project.

3.3.4 THE REQUIRED FACILITIES AND EQUIPMENT

The project will be carried out mainly on the premises of the Santa Cruz Asset. Existing equipment and resources will be used.

3.4 PROGRAMMING AND ORGANIZATION OF THE PROJECT

The project activities are organised in four phases. Each one of these groups a set of activities, which can be seen in detail in the activity programming section. The phases of the project are as shown in Figure 12.

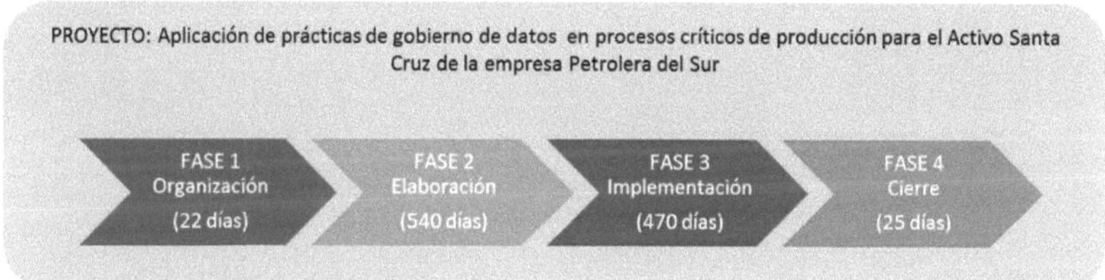

Figure 12: Schematic of project phases
Source: Own elaboration.

3.4.1 PROGRAMMING OF ACTIVITIES

A detailed schedule of activities is provided in section [**6.1 Annex I**] of this document, which groups the activities by phase and group of activity. The schedule also includes a Gantt chart containing the task dependency and specifying the critical path of the project (red bars on the Gantt).

3.4.2 ORGANISATION FOR THE OPERATION OF THE PROJECT

For the execution of the schedule of activities set out in the previous section, a work team will be formed with the following actors:

- **Sponsor**: Project sponsor. It is responsible for ensuring the availability of resources and the formalisation of the project at company level.
- **External Consultant**: Certified specialist in data governance system implementation processes.
- **Team leader**: This role will be assumed by the data manager of Activo Santa Cruz.
- **Project manager**: This role will be assumed by the project management office of Activo Santa Cruz.
- **Petrolera del Sur's Production Management** Company Data Manager: The company's data manager, external to the Asset, who will collaborate throughout the project and at the same time will be responsible for certifying its training in the "*Training*" stage of the project.

- **Data manager of Activo Neuquén**: Same as data manager of Gcia. de Gace. de producción de Petrolera del Sur.
- **IT Analyst**: Same as Production Manager of Petrolera del Sur.
- **Process analyst**: IT professional with experience and ability to survey and map work processes with BPM and BPMN methodology.
- **IT analyst/s specialists**: Technical specialists in the various IT disciplines who will be involved in the project at the specific times required.

Within the work team we can observe a combination of resources, we have those who are part of the organization of the Asset and others that belong to the general scope of the company, coming from sectors or areas that have a close relationship with the characteristics of the project. In the team organization scheme shown in Figure 13 we can see how the staff outside the Asset continues to depend on their respective management.
Throughout the project, the team, in the role of project manager, will apply all known good practices in this discipline. Great importance will also be given to the communication strategy to be implemented during the project, considering the application of all the formal and informal means existing in the company.

Figure 13: **Organisational diagram** of the **work team**
Source: Own elaboration.

3.4.3 ENTITY RESPONSIBLE FOR IMPLEMENTATION

The responsibility for the implementation of the project will lie with Santa Cruz Asset Management. The asset will provide "full-time" allocation to the asset data manager (Team Leader), "part-time" allocation to the project manager and the asset manager will assume sponsorship of the project, also with a "part-time" allocation. See Figure 19.
Resources outside the Assets will have a "part-time" type allocation with significant workload in the "Development" and "Implementation" phases.

3.5 FINANCIAL ASPECTS OF THE PROJECT

3.5.1 PROJECT COSTS

The project costs will be classified according to the following concepts

- **External Consultancy**: This item includes the amounts invested in external consultancy.
- **IT Services**: This includes the amounts invested in internal consultancy activities that will be required from the company's IT area.
- **Training and certification of personnel**: The amounts invested in training and education activities for the company's own personnel, assets and the company are considered.
- **Logistics**: This item groups together the amounts needed to invest in travel, accommodation and organisation of the activities involved in the project.

All these concepts correspond to fixed investment. No investment in working capital is required given the nature and structure of this project. There are no plans to incorporate new personnel or acquire physical assets.
The operation/production costs are considered from year three onwards, since according to the analysis carried out it is from this period that the benefits begin to be generated.

3.5.1.1 FIXED INVESTMENT AND PRODUCTION COSTS

Table 28 details the fixed investment amounts earmarked for the project. These are classified according to the concepts mentioned above and are specified in greater detail. The production costs are estimated considering the cost per unit of production projected for the periods in which the income / benefits are executed, for the incremental production units that are estimated to be obtained. The taxes considered with:

- **Royalties**: For the province of Santa Cruz, the rate is **12% of the** gross profits generated by the activity.
- **Gross income**: A rate of **1% is** considered on the gross profits generated by the activity.
- **Income tax**: A rate of **37% is** considered on net profits generated by the activity.

Table 28: Details of fixed investment required to implement the project

Concepto de Inversión fija / Detalles	Monto U$S (Dólares)
Formación (1)	
Gestor de datos - Activo Santa Cruz	4,000
Gestor de datos - Gerencia de producción Compania	4,000
Gestor de datos - Otro Activo	4,000
Analista funcional TI	4,000
Sub total Formación	**16,000**
Consultoría Externa (2)	
Consultoría etapa 1	66,900
Consultoría etapa 2	66,900
Sub total Consultoría Externa	**133,800**
Servicios TI (3)	
Analista consultor de procesos	4,700
Analista consultor especialista	10,000
Analista funcional	36,000
Sub total Servicios TI	**50,700**
Logística (4)	
Viajes	20,800
Estadía	46,800
Capacitación	1,500
Sub total Logística	**69,100**
Total inversión fija	**269,600**

Note: Source: The data displayed in the table are produced by the company.

(1) The training includes the costs of certification (**US$ 1500 per person)** and the purchase of the training material (**US$ 2500 per person**). The project plans to train and certify four members of the company, of which three are from the E&P area (one from Activo Santa Cruz) and the remaining from the IT area.

(2) For external consultancy, the participation of a consultant specialised in this type of project is considered. It is expected that the consultant will come from abroad, from the United States or England, since these are the countries where the best trained and most experienced resources are found. The service was considered in two stages, both lasting thirty days at the facilities of Activo Santa Cruz.

(3) The cost per hour of each person in the company's IT area is considered. The working modality of this area is to transfer the costs of the personnel to the projects and business areas in which they participate.

(4) The logistics take into account all travel and living expenses of the team designated for the project. Expenses in this same concept of external consultancy are excluded.

3.5.1.2 TIMELINE OF COSTS

In Table 29 we can see the chronology of costs according to the organisation of the project.

Table 29: Cost chronology by period

Año Período	Valores sin descontar Expresados en [U$S]	Concepto
0	16,000	Inversión fija
1	116,133	Inversión fija
2	34,533	Inversión fija
3	2,761,410	Inversión fija + Costos de operación y producción
4	1,715,932	Costos de operación y producción
Total	**4,644,008**	

Note: Source: The data displayed in the table are produced by the company.

3.5.2 INCOME OR PROFITS FROM THE PROJECT

The income or benefits of the project are considered through the positive impact that is expected to be generated in the process: "*Process of determining and monitoring the causes of production losses*", which will have a direct impact on production, increasing it.

To estimate the profit, the percentage impact of the lost production volumes on the production potential of the Asset for each of its products was considered. This variable is one of the indicators that allow you to evaluate your management. The project expects to reduce this percentage to seven percent (**7%) in the** case of gas. In the case of oil and gasoline production, it is expected to decrease this percentage to nine percent (**9%**). This decrease, as we mentioned before, leads to an increase in the production of both gas and oil and gasoline, which generates more income.

The basis of the estimate lies in the impact observed in this process in recent years, during which a series of activities associated with the data management discipline have been developed, which, in line with the Asset strategy, have led to an improvement in the indicators (see section [**6.4 Annex IV**]). This is sustained over time and we believe that it will be further developed as the project is implemented. Figure 14 shows the change in trend over this period in the case of gas losses. To a lesser extent, Figure 15 shows this for oil losses; in this case, although no change in the trend is observed, we identified an opportunity scenario that the project intends to take advantage of, seeking to reverse the trend as with gas losses.

In implementing the project and considering that the new data governance practices will be applied in the processes achieved, it is expected that from the third year of the project's life the above-mentioned benefits will start to materialize.

In the rest of the processes achieved, it is also expected that benefits will be obtained. These will be evaluated by means of variables of a qualitative nature, focusing on the efficiency of the work processes in which data are handled. The variables will be defined within the project as well as the monitoring structure that supports them.

Another benefit associated with the project is to try to establish relationships between qualitative benefits and business results and thus find support for future projects.

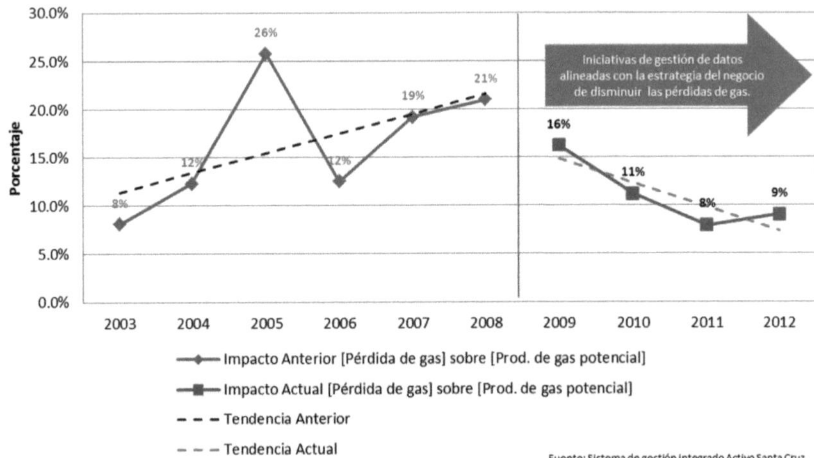

Figure 14: Gas loss impact graph
Source: Own elaboration with data obtained from the source indicated in the figure.

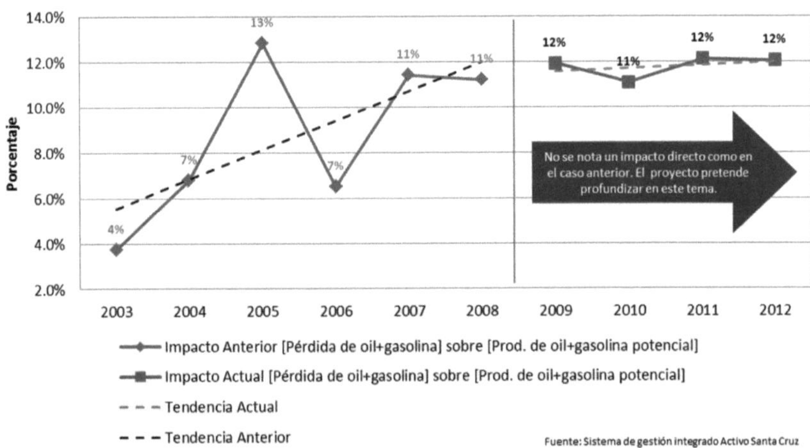

Figure 15: Impact graph of liquid hydrocarbon losses
Source: Own elaboration with data obtained from the source indicated in the figure.

3.5.2.1 PROJECT INCOME

The values considered to quantify the project's income are the product of the increase in production due to the cost of selling it on the market.

3.5.2.2 INCOME CHRONOLOGY

In Table 30 we present the chronology of income throughout the project.

Table 30: Income chronology by period

Año Período	Valores sin descontar Expresados en [U$S]	Concepto
0	0	No se generan ingresos
1	0	No se generan ingresos
2	0	No se generan ingresos
3	3,059,436	Venta de gas + petróleo y gasolina.
4	1,875,579	Venta de gas + petróleo y gasolina.
Total	**4,935,015**	

Note: Source: The data displayed in the table are produced by the company.

3.5.2.3 CASH FLOW

Table 31, based on all the data presented above, presents the cash flow of the project.

Table 31: Project cash flow. Expressed in dollars [U$S] for periods of one year

Concepto / Detalle	Año 1	Año 2	Año 3	Año 4
Ingresos				
Capital inicial invertido	269,600	0	0	0
Saldo año anterior	0	137,467	102,933	400,960
Ventas de Gas	0	0	793,354	574,928
Ventas de petróleo y gasolina	0	0	2,266,082	1,300,652
Total de Ingresos	**269,600**	**137,467**	**3,162,370**	**2,276,539**
Gastos				
Inversión	132,133	34,533	102,933	0
Gastos de producción	0	0	2,025,265	1,378,345
Total gastos	**132,133**	**34,533**	**2,128,199**	**1,378,345**
Impuestos				
Regalias [12%]	0	0	367,132	225,069
Ingresos Brutos [1%]	0	0	30,594	18,756
Ganancias [37%]	0	0	235,484	93,761
Total Impuestos	**0**	**0**	**633,211**	**337,587**
Saldo a ser transferido	**137,467**	**102,933**	**400,960**	**560,607**

Note: Source: The data displayed in the table are produced by the company.

As can be seen from the table above, the **benefits of the project at the end of the project will be a cash balance of US$560,607 or its equivalent in national currency**.

3.5.3 SOURCES OF FUNDING

Due to the characteristics of the project and considering that the amount to be invested does not represent an obstacle for the budget of the Asset and added to the financial strategy, which establishes that in the last years the company has decided to execute the investment projects with its own resources, it will not require external financing sources
The total amount to be invested is **U$S 269,600,** which will be invested during the first three years of the project. See details in Table 28.

3.6 FINANCIAL EVALUATION AND RISKS

3.6.1 NET PRESENT VALUE

The Net Present Value (NPV) of a project is defined as the value obtained by updating, separately for each period of the project's duration, the difference between all the cash income and expenses that occur during the life of a project at a predetermined fixed interest rate.
Applying a discount rate of **15.3%,** this rate is the one applied by the company to evaluate its project portfolio, the Net Present Value of the net benefits of the Project amounts to **U$S 142,065**. The Benefit-Cost ratio gives a coefficient of **U$S 1.05, which** means that for every dollar invested I get an additional U$S 1.05, which is a good proportion for a project of these characteristics. In Table 32 we can detail the values that support the values expressed above.

Table 32: Financial Evaluation [US$ amounts] - Net Present Value Discount rate 15.3%.

Año	Valores sin descontar			Valores descontados		
	Costos	Beneficios	Beneficios Netos	Costos	Beneficios	Beneficios Netos
0	16,000	0	-16,000	16,000	0	-16,000
1	116,133	0	-116,133	100,723	0	-100,723
2	34,533	0	-34,533	25,976	0	-25,976
3	2,761,410	3,059,436	298,027	1,801,536	1,995,968	194,432
4	1,715,932	1,875,579	159,648	970,918	1,061,251	90,333
Total	4,644,008	4,935,015	291,007	2,915,153	3,057,219	142,065
	Relación Beneficio/Costo	1.05	**VAN**	142,065	**TIR**	56.5%

Note: Source: The data displayed in the table are produced by the company.

3.6.2 TIR - INTERNAL RATE OF RETURN

The project's internal rate of return is **56.5%**. The values considered in the calculation can be found in Table 32.

3.6.3 MOST IMPORTANT RISKS

If we base ourselves on the historical background and focus on the causes that prevented the execution of other similar projects in the company, we can mention the following aspects with the risk category:

I. **Risks of organizational change**: Organizational changes, in most cases, derive from changes in strategy of the executing organization. Petrolera del Sur has not been unaware of this scenario and in these cases the execution and/or evaluation of innovative projects have always been affected, mainly because this type of change generates a time of reordering and adaptation of the organization to the new strategy.

II. **Risks associated with the size of the project**: Earlier projects had a wider scope, which made it difficult to gain political support within the organisation.

III. **Risks associated with aspects of the relationship between different organisational areas**: The relations between the IT area and the operational areas of the business have not provided (except for specific exceptions) a suitable scenario for carrying out this type of project. Political and competition aspects have had a negative influence.

IV. **Risks associated with the country's political and economic context**: Experience indicates that the country's political and economic context also generates uncertainty within organizations. Petrolera del Sur is no exception, the context sometimes does not generate the necessary confidence for companies to feel secure in investing in innovation projects.

V. **Risks associated with the rotation of personnel in the** industry: In recent years, the shortage of human resources dedicated to the industry in which Petrolera del Sur operates has generated a high rotation of people between different companies. This aspect has a negative impact when key resources involved in a current project or in an execution plan are lost.

To mitigate these risks, the following mitigating measures were taken in the planning and evaluation of this project

I. **Risks of organisational change**: Giving the project the character of a pilot, with a scope limited to the operational limits of an asset that has already been working on these issues informally and with results that can be perceived, is a way of mitigating this type of risk. Considering a quantitative measure of the benefits committed to the project also helps to mitigate the risk. It is very difficult for an organisation not to consider a project that can demonstrate its results quantitatively and qualitatively.

II. **Risks associated with the size of the project**: The project covers four critical processes of Activo Santa Cruz. It is not considered to incorporate more technology than is available, nor is it considered to increase the number of its own staff. Everything revolves around adopting new management practices. The amounts to be invested have a very low impact on the Asset's investment budget and all the precedents of previous similar initiatives were considered. All these measures allow us to mitigate the risk that the scope of the project is considered to be of an inappropriate size for the current context of the organisation.

III. **Risks associated with aspects of the relationship between different organisational areas**: Throughout the feasibility study and also from the experience gathered, we can confirm that Activo Santa Cruz has maintained a positive and synergistic relationship with the IT area. The project will be executed by a team made up of human resources from both areas. The proposed team expects to have people who have already been working on these issues together.

IV. **Risks associated to the country's political and economic context**: Although the country's political and economic context is influenced by the current electoral moment, it is also true that any type of initiative that favours an increase in the production and commercialisation of hydrocarbons has a high impact, both in the company's internal context and in the national context, given that imports of this product have been rising steadily.

V. **Risks associated with the rotation of personnel in the industry**: A strategy was developed in conjunction with the human resources areas that will allow us to minimise this risk. This consists of a commitment act between Petrolera del Sur and the personnel involved in the project, which would specify the organisation's willingness to invest in the training and execution of this project and the personnel would commit to remaining in the company during the time that the project is developed. The act would include exception clauses for situations of force majeure for both parties. This type of agreement already exists and applies to cases in which the organisation invests in postgraduate training for its own staff.

3.7 CONCLUSIONS AND RECOMMENDATIONS

The proposed project incorporates, formalizes and promotes data management practices that will allow Activo Santa Cruz and the Southern Oil Company to obtain improvements in management and results.

The profit trigger is based on the reduction of production losses and their consequent impact on production increases. It also represents the point of greatest sensitivity of the project. We recommend carrying out a sensitivity analysis if you decide to implement it.

This project will lay the foundation for the development of data management as a necessary and fundamental discipline for achieving business objectives at all levels of the organization.

The scenario described represents a favourable environment; the Asset and the Company have the necessary strengths to exploit all the opportunities that were dimensioned in this project. The weaknesses and threats were considered in the conception of this project and do not represent risks that prevent its execution.

It seems that we recommend to execute the project in Activo Santa Cruz, we consider that there is a suitable environment for its execution. It is also profitable because it has a **NPV (Net Present Value) of US$ 142,065,** a benefit-cost ratio of US$ **1.05 and** an **IRR of 56.5%**.

4 ANNEXES

4.1 ANNEX I - PROJECT SCHEDULE

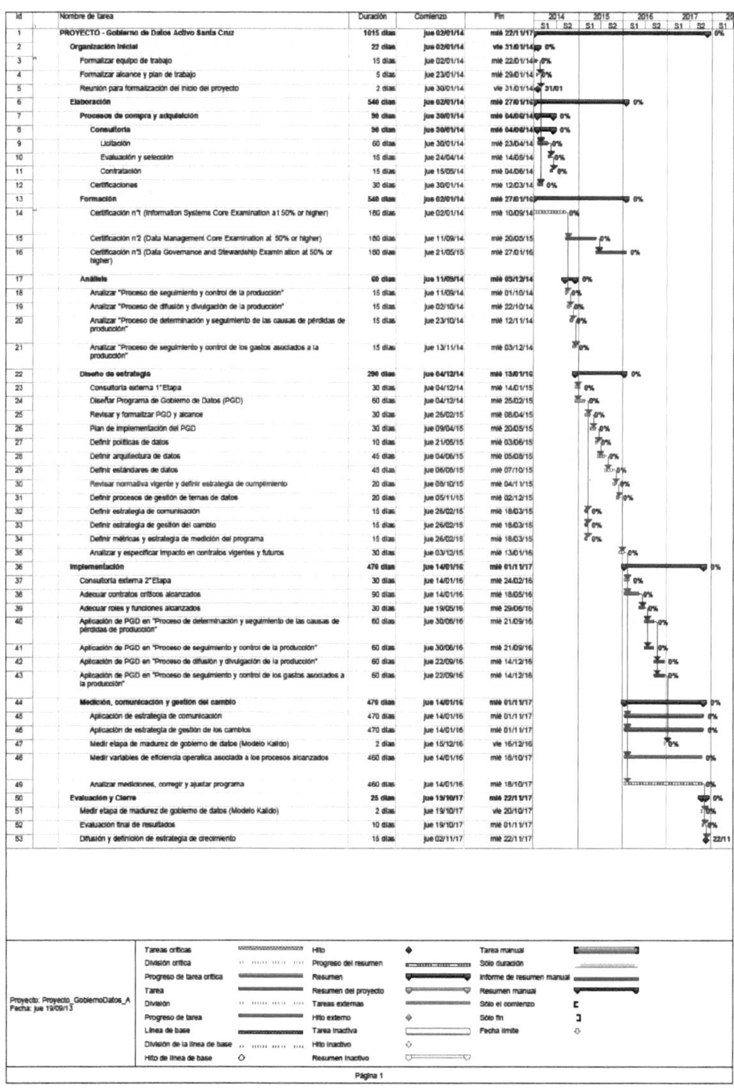

Id	Nombre de tarea	Duración	Comienzo	Fin
1	**PROYECTO - Gobierno de Datos Activo Santa Cruz**	**1015 días**	**jue 02/01/14**	**mié 22/11/17**
2	**Organización Inicial**	**22 días**	**jue 02/01/14**	**vie 31/01/14**
3	Formalizar equipo de trabajo	15 días	jue 02/01/14	mié 22/01/14
4	Formalizar alcance y plan de trabajo	5 días	jue 23/01/14	mié 29/01/14
5	Reunión para formalización del inicio del proyecto	2 días	jue 30/01/14	vie 31/01/14
6	**Elaboración**	**540 días**	**jue 02/01/14**	**mié 27/01/16**
7	**Procesos de compra y adquisición**	**90 días**	**jue 30/01/14**	**mié 04/06/14**
8	**Consultoría**	**90 días**	**jue 30/01/14**	**mié 04/06/14**
9	Licitación	60 días	jue 30/01/14	mié 23/04/14
10	Evaluación y selección	15 días	jue 24/04/14	mié 14/05/14
11	Contratación	15 días	jue 15/05/14	mié 04/06/14
12	**Certificaciones**	30 días	jue 30/01/14	mié 12/03/14
13	**Formación**	**540 días**	**jue 02/01/14**	**mié 27/01/16**
14	Certificación n°1 (Information Systems Core Examination at 50% or higher)	180 días	jue 02/01/14	mié 10/09/14
15	Certificación n°2 (Data Management Core Examination at 50% or higher)	180 días	jue 11/09/14	mié 20/05/15
16	Certificación n°3 (Data Governance and Stewardship Examin ation at 50% or higher)	180 días	jue 21/05/15	mié 27/01/16
17	**Análisis**	**60 días**	**jue 11/09/14**	**mié 03/12/14**
18	Analizar "Proceso de seguimiento y control de la producción"	15 días	jue 11/09/14	mié 01/10/14
19	Analizar "Proceso de difusión y divulgación de la producción"	15 días	jue 02/10/14	mié 22/10/14
20	Analizar "Proceso de determinación y seguimiento de las causas de pérdidas de producción"	15 días	jue 23/10/14	mié 12/11/14
21	Analizar "Proceso de seguimiento y control de los gastos asociados a la producción"	15 días	jue 13/11/14	mié 03/12/14
22	**Diseño de estrategia**	**290 días**	**jue 04/12/14**	**mié 13/01/16**
23	Consultoría externa 1°Etapa	30 días	jue 04/12/14	mié 14/01/15
24	Diseñar Programa de Gobierno de Datos (PGD)	60 días	jue 04/12/14	mié 25/02/15
25	Revisar y formalizar PGD y alcance	30 días	jue 26/02/15	mié 08/04/15
26	Plan de implementación del PGD	30 días	jue 09/04/15	mié 20/05/15
27	Definir políticas de datos	10 días	jue 21/05/15	mié 03/06/15
28	Definir arquitectura de datos	45 días	jue 04/06/15	mié 05/08/15
29	Definir estándares de datos	45 días	jue 06/08/15	mié 07/10/15
30	Revisar normativa vigente y definir estrategia de cumplimiento	20 días	jue 08/10/15	mié 04/11/15
31	Definir procesos de gestión de temas de datos	20 días	jue 05/11/15	mié 02/12/15
32	Definir estrategia de comunicación	15 días	jue 26/02/15	mié 18/03/15
33	Definir estrategia de gestión del cambio	15 días	jue 26/02/15	mié 18/03/15
34	Definir métricas y estrategia de medición del programa	15 días	jue 26/02/15	mié 18/03/15
35	Analizar y especificar impacto en contratos vigentes y futuros	30 días	jue 03/12/15	mié 13/01/16
36	**Implementación**	**470 días**	**jue 14/01/16**	**mié 01/11/17**
37	Consultoría externa 2°Etapa	30 días	jue 14/01/16	mié 24/02/16
38	Adecuar contratos críticos alcanzados	90 días	jue 14/01/16	mié 18/05/16
39	Adecuar roles y funciones alcanzados	30 días	jue 19/05/16	mié 29/06/16
40	Aplicación de PGD en "Proceso de determinación y seguimiento de las causas de pérdidas de producción"	60 días	jue 30/06/16	mié 21/09/16
41	Aplicación de PGD en "Proceso de seguimiento y control de la producción"	60 días	jue 30/06/16	mié 21/09/16
42	Aplicación de PGD en "Proceso de difusión y divulgación de la producción"	60 días	jue 22/09/16	mié 14/12/16
43	Aplicación de PGD en "Proceso de seguimiento y control de los gastos asociados a la producción"	60 días	jue 22/09/16	mié 14/12/16
44	**Medición, comunicación y gestión del cambio**	**470 días**	**jue 14/01/16**	**mié 01/11/17**
45	Aplicación de estrategia de comunicación	470 días	jue 14/01/16	mié 01/11/17
46	Aplicación de estrategia de gestión de los cambios	470 días	jue 14/01/16	mié 01/11/17
47	Medir etapa de madurez de gobierno de datos (Modelo Kalido)	2 días	jue 15/12/16	vie 16/12/16
48	Medir variables de eficiencia operativa asociada a los procesos alcanzados	460 días	jue 14/01/16	mié 18/10/17
49	Analizar mediciones, corregir y ajustar programa	460 días	jue 14/01/16	mié 18/10/17
50	**Evaluación y Cierre**	**25 días**	**jue 19/10/17**	**mié 22/11/17**
51	Medir etapa de madurez de gobierno de datos (Modelo Kalido)	2 días	jue 19/10/17	vie 20/10/17
52	Evaluación final de resultados	10 días	jue 19/10/17	mié 01/11/17
53	Difusión y definición de estrategia de crecimiento	15 días	jue 02/11/17	mié 22/11/17

4.2 ANNEX II - PROCESS MAP

In Figure 16 we can see an example of a process section mapped with the BPMN symbol that we will use for the project. This is a technique already known by the company and at the same time there is computer technology that facilitates the documentation process.

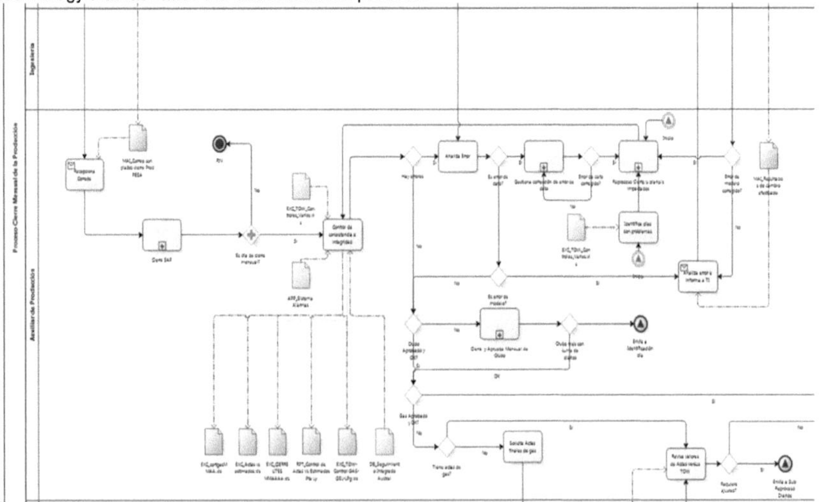

Figure 16: Example of a process map

4.3 ANNEX III - RECIENT MATRIX

In Figure 17 we present an example of the structure that has a RECI matrix.

Matriz RECI

ROLES	
R	Responsable
E	Ejecuta
C	Consultado
I	Informado
R,E	Responsable y ejecuta

						Activo Santa Cruz				E&P Petrolera Santa Cruz				Externos
						Producción			Ingeniería	Otros Sectores				Externos
						Auxiliar de Producción	Gerente de Producción	Líder de Polo	Ingeniería	Contabilidad	Gerencia de Producción PESA	Relación con Gobiernos y Socios	TI	IESC
	Entradas	**Desde Etapa N°**	**Descripción**	**Hasta Etapa N°**	**Salidas**	**ROLES**								
1	Requisitos Organizacionales										R			
2		-	Envia Plazos establecidos para cierre	5		I	I				R	E		C
3					MAI_Correo con plazos cierre Prod PESA									
4	Requisitos Organizacionales										R			
5		2	Inicia el proceso de cierre de producción	7		E	R			I				
6					MAI_Correo con plazos cierre Logístico PESA	E	I			R				
7		5	Cierre SAP	17		E	R							
8					MAI_Correo notificando cierre definitivo de la producción en SAP	E	R			I				

Figure 17: Example of a RECI matrix model

4.4 ANNEX IV - IMPACT OF DATA MANAGEMENT INITIATIVES ON GAS PRODUCTION LOSSES

Since 2008 and in line with the strategy of the Asset Operations Management, which aimed to improve operational efficiency, work has been started on analysing historical and current data on production losses. These were of concern because they showed an increasing trend in their evolution. The following shortcomings associated with aspects of data management were identified from the analysis:

1. The classification of losses, the context in which they occurred, was not always correct. In many cases these were classified with very general criteria that did not allow to identify the real cause of the problems.
2. Access to loss data was not simple and the people who, because of their function, had to analyse and make preventive decisions about the problems that generated them, spent a great deal of time manipulating and classifying the data in order to generate information to support their decisions.
3. There were no formal performance indicators for the various production units that would allow specific targets to be set for reducing losses by production poles, for example. This also made it difficult to include associated personal performance targets.
4. The contracts with the service companies did not specify the degree of responsibility for production losses.

Data management principles were applied and the following results were achieved

1. Work was done on the people who identified and recorded the losses. The impact of not correctly recording the causes of the stoppages was explained to them through training and with objective data. The results were very good. In three years the volume of unclassified losses was reduced from **27%** to **5%**. See Figure 18.

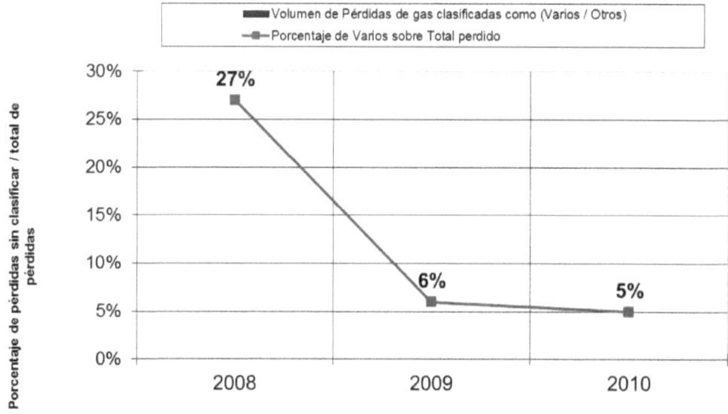

Figure 18: Evolution of the volume of losses without an identified cause

2. Through the use of IT (Available and not exploited to its full potential) solutions were built that provided the appropriate personnel with timely and accurate access to loss data and information, classified and prepared for analysis. A series of indicators were built to measure the management of losses per unit of production at all necessary levels of aggregation.

3. By defining a set of production loss indicators, consensus was built on how to calculate and display them, these same indicators were used to set abatement targets for all levels of the organization with responsibility for production, these were also reflected in people's performance objectives. The

conceptual model used to generate, visualize and analyze the indicators is the one shown in Figure 19.

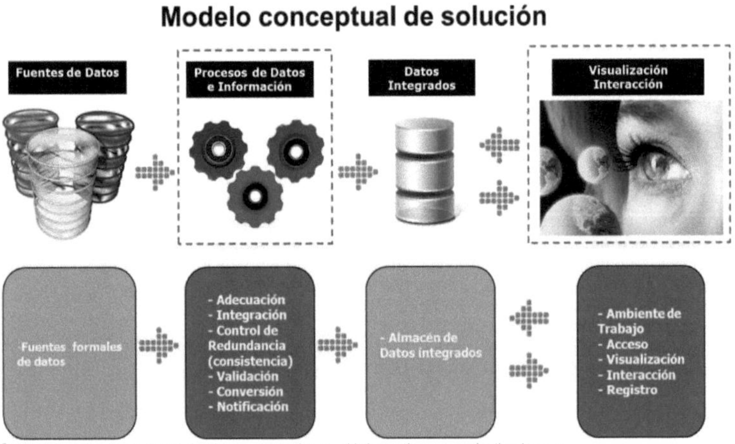

Modelo conceptual de solución

Fuentes de Datos
Procesos de Datos e Información
Datos Integrados
Visualización Interacción

Fuentes formales de datos
- Adecuación
- Integración
- Control de Redundancia (consistencia)
- Validación
- Conversión
- Notificación
- Almacén de Datos integrados
- Ambiente de Trabajo
- Acceso
- Visualización
- Interacción
- Registro

Figure 19: Model solution to facilitate timely access to data and information on production losses

4. The high decision levels of the service companies were involved and shown with objective data the impact of losses and how these not only impact on the results of the company operating the Asset. Staff were trained in the criteria for classifying losses. With one company we even built a data interface between our own information system and that of Petrolera del Sur. This led to the elimination of redundant data loading work, focusing on control and analysis.

By way of conclusion we can say the following:

I. The problem was addressed by considering the elements involved in the data governance function:
   Processes: The process was reviewed. Data manipulation activities, roles and functions involved, tools used, etc. were identified.
   People: Own and third party staff were trained and engaged on loss classification criteria, processes for obtaining and classifying data and information, and were involved in all consensus-building and needs-defining activities.
   Technology: The use of available technology was maximised.

II. The data strategy accompanied the business strategy and the impact was remarkable and constant over time.
III. It is not possible to say exactly to what extent the results were impacted, if there is a conviction that the impact was positive.
IV. The focus was on gas leaks.

5 BIBLIOGRAPHY

[1] MOSLEY, M., BRACKETT, M., EARLEY, S. y HENDERSON, D., The DAMA Guide to The Data Management Body of Knowledge (DAMA-DMBOOK Guide), NJ 07720 U.S.A.: Technics Publications, LLC, 2009.

[2] LLANOA, P., "Governance for all," 07 12 2011. [Online]. Available: http://www.americaeconomia.com/analisis-opinion/governance-para-todos. Last accessed: 15 07 2013].

[3] WIKIPEDIA, "Business Process Management," 30 10 2014. [Online]. Available: http://es.wikipedia.org/wiki/Gesti%C3%B3n_de_procesos_de_negocio. [Last access: 08 11 2014].

[4] WIKIPEDIA, "Business Process Model and Notation," 24 09 2014. [Online]. Available: http://es.wikipedia.org/wiki/Business_Process_Modeling_Notation. [Last accessed: 08 11 2014].

[5] BIZAGI, "Application for BPM in Petrolera del Sur," 08 11 2014. [On line]. Available: http://www.bizagi.com/es. [Last access: 05 05 2013].

[6] PÉREZ FERNÁNDEZ DE VELAZCO, JOSÉ A., GESTION POR PROCESOS (Como utilizar ISO 9001:2000 para mejorar la gestión de la Organización), Madrid: ESIC Editorial, 2004.

[7] INTERNATIONAL LABOUR OFFICE, "Basic Guide for the Preparation of Project Profiles," 2004. [On line]. Available: http://www.ilo.org/ipec/Informationresources/WCMS_IPEC_PUB_7147/lang--es/index.htm. Last accessed: 05 05 2013].

[8] DISTEFANO, G., *EVALUACIÓN INTEGRAL* DEL *ACTIVO SANTA CRUZ,* Río Gallegos, Santa Cruz: Petrolera del Sur, 2008.

[9] OLMO, C., VELAZCO, R., "Experiences of data quality evaluation," *Petrotecnia,* pp. 52-61, 2011.

[10] DGI, "The Data Governance Institute (DGI)," 08 11 2014. Online]. Available: http://www.datagovernance.com/. [Last accessed: 05 05 2013].

[11] MC CARTHY, K., "Data Governance KPIs," 28 02 2012. [Online]. [Last accessed: 05 05 2013].

[12] NASCIO Staff, "Data Governance Part II: Maturity Models - A Path to Progress," 03 2009. [En línea]. Available: http://www.nascio.org/publications/documents/NASCIO-DataGovernancePTII.pdf. [Último acceso: 05 05 2013].

[13] FERNANDEZ CIRELLI, A., The Technological Entrepreneur, EUDEBA, 1996.

[14] OLMO, C., VELAZCO, R., *METHODOLOGY FOR CONTINUOUS IMPROVEMENT OF INFORMATION TREATMENT PROCESSES, Buenos Aires,* Buenos Aires: Petrolera del Sur, 2010.

[15] WINSTON, CH., "Kalido Data Governance Maturity Assessment Report," Kalido, Rio Gallegos, 2011.

[16] NASCIO Staff, "Data Governance - Managing Information As An Enterprise Asset Part I - An Introduction," 04 2008. [En línea]. Available: http://www.nascio.org/publications/documents/NASCIO-DataGovernance-Part1.pdf. [Último acceso: 05 05 2013].

[17] SEINER, ROBERT S., "The Data Stewardship Approach to Data Governance: Chapter 1," 01 2006. [En línea]. Available: http://www.tdan.com/view-articles/5037. [Último acceso: 05 05 2013].

[18] SEINER, ROBERT S., "The Data Stewardship Approach to Data Governance: Chapter 2," 04 2006. [En línea]. Available: http://www.tdan.com/view-articles/5029. [Último acceso: 05 05 2013].

[19] SEINER, ROBERT S., "The Data Stewardship Approach to Data Governance: Chapter 3," 10 2006. [En línea]. Available: http://www.tdan.com/view-articles/4042. [Último acceso: 05 05 2013].

[20] SEINER, ROBERT S., "The Data Stewardship Approach to Data Governance: Chapter 4," 01 2007. [En línea]. Available: http://www.tdan.com/view-articles/4427. [Último acceso: 05 05 2013].

[21] SEINER, ROBERT S., "The Data Stewardship Approach to Data Governance: Chapter 5," 04 2007. [En línea]. Available: http://www.tdan.com/view-articles/4429. [Último acceso: 05 05 2013].

[22] SEINER, ROBERT S., "The Data Stewardship Approach to Data Governance: Chapter 6," 07 2007. [En línea]. Available: http://www.tdan.com/view-articles/5604. [Último acceso: 05 05 2013].

[23] SEINER, ROBERT S., "The Data Stewardship Approach to Data Governance: Chapter 7," 10 2007. [En línea]. Available: http://www.tdan.com/view-articles/6173. [Último acceso: 05 05 2013].

[24] SEINER, ROBERT S., "The Data Stewardship Approach to Data Governance: Chapter 8," 16 02 2008. [En línea]. Available: http://www.tdan.com/view-articles/6703. [Último acceso: 05 05 2013].

[25] SEINER, ROBERT S., "The Data Stewardship Approach to Data Governance: Part 9," 08 2008. [En línea]. Available: http://www.tdan.com/view-articles/7596. [Último acceso: 05 05 2013].

[26] SEINER, ROBERT S., "The Data Stewardship Approach to Data Governance: Part 10," 02 2009. [En línea]. Available: http://www.tdan.com/view-articles/9610. [Último acceso: 05 05 2013].

[27] NASCIO, "National Association of State Chief Information Officers (NASCIO)," 1969. [En línea]. Available: http://www.nascio.org/. [Último acceso: 05 05 2013].

[28] NASCIO Staff, "Data Governance Part III: Frameworks - Structure for Organizing Complexity," 05 2009. [En línea]. Available: http://www.nascio.org/publications/documents/NASCIO-DataGovernancePTIII.pdf. [Último acceso: 05 05 2013].

[29] NASCIO Staff, "IT Governance and Business Outcomes - A Shared Responsibility between IT and Business Leadership," 03 2008. [En línea]. Available: http://www.nascio.org/publications/documents/NASCIO-ITGovernanceBusinessOutcomes.pdf. [Último acceso: 05 05 2013].

[30] NASCIO Staff, "ENTERPRISE ARCHITECTURE - THE PATH TO GOVERNMENT TRANSFORMATION," 10 2005. [On line]. Available: http://www.nascio.org/publications/documents/NASCIO-eaAssessment.pdf. [Last accessed: 05 05 2013].

[31] NASCIO Staff, "A Blueprint for Better Government: The Information Sharing Imperative," 05 2005. [En línea]. Available: http://www.nascio.org/advocacy/dcFlyIn/callForAction05.pdf. [Último acceso: 05 05 2013].

[32] NASCIO Staff, "Government Information Sharing: Calls to Action," 03 2005. [En línea]. Available: http://www.nascio.org/publications/documents/NASCIO-Perspectives.pdf. [Último acceso: 05 05 2013].

[33] NASCIO Staff, "We Need to Talk: Governance Models to Advance Communications Interoperability," 11 2005. [En línea]. Available: http://www.nascio.org/publications/documents/NASCIO-InteropGovResearchBrief.pdf. [Último acceso: 05 05 2013].

[34] NASCIO Staff, "A National Framework for Collaborative Information Exchange: What is NIEM?," 03 2006. [En línea]. Available: http://www.nascio.org/publications/documents/NASCIO-National_Information_Exchange_Model_Initiative.pdf. [Último acceso: 05 05 2013].

[35] CISR, "Center for Information Systems Research," 08 11 2014. [Online]. Available: http://cisr.mit.edu/. Last access: 05 05 2013].

[36] DAMA, "DAMA International," 08 11 2014. [On line]. Available: http://www.dama.org/. Last accessed: 05 05 2013].

[37] ITGI, "The IT Governance Institute (ITGI)," 08 11 2014. [On line]. Available: http://www.itgi.org/. [Last accessed: 05 05 2013].

[38] ISACA, "Information Systems Audit and Control Association (ISACA)," 08 11 2014. [En línea]. Available: https://www.isaca.org/Pages/default.aspx. [Último acceso: 05 05 2013].

[39] NIEM, "The National Information Exchange Model (NIEM)," 08 11 2014. Online]. Available: https://www.niem.gov/Pages/default.aspx. Last accessed: 05 05 2013.

[40] GEORGES, D., "Data Governance: A Six-Step Solution," 02 09 2010. [On line]. Available: http://www.realcomm.com/advisory/advisory.asp?AdvisoryID=439. Last accessed on: 05 05 2013].

[41] State Geospatial Data Governance Work Group, "Geospatial Data Governance Plan (GIS Project)," 16 11 2010. [En línea]. Available: http://www.colorado.gov/cs/Satellite?c=Document_C&childpagename=OIT-EADG%2FDocument_C%2FCBONAddLinkView&cid=1251591162198&pagename=CBONWrapper. [Último acceso: 05 05 2013].

[42] DUVALL, L., "Jump Starting Data Governance: a Program Manager's Story," 13 07 2011. [Online]. Available: http://mitiq.mit.edu/IQIS/Documents/CDOIQS_201177/Papers/02_04_1C-1_Duvall.pdf. Last accessed: 05 05 2013].

[43] LAIRD, E., RYAN, R., "Data Governance: Changing Culture, Breaking Down Silos, and Deciding Who is in Control," 28 08 2008. [En línea]. Available: http://www.dataqualitycampaign.org/files/events/resources/meetings-dqc_quarterly_issue_brief-072908.pdf. [Último acceso: 05 05 2013].

[44] INFORMATION BUILDERS, "Building a Business Case for," [En línea]. Available: http://www.informationbuilders.com/sites/www.informationbuilders.com/files/pdf/about_us/whitepapers/wp_businesscasefordgtencriticalsteps_iway_2012_0.pdf. [Último acceso: 05 05 2013].

Printed by Books on Demand GmbH, Norderstedt / Germany